Free Sermons: The ... for Modern Times

By
Patrick Doucette

FOURTH EDITION

* * * * *

Free Sermons: The Best Free Sermons for Modern Times

Copyright © 2015 Patrick Doucette

*****

Introduction and dedication:

Thank you for choosing this book. You may freely use these sermons and modify them for your own purpose as needed. This book is dedicated to all those who search for truth, the author hopes it will be an encouragement and a blessing to anyone and everyone who may take the time to read and absorb the words contained herein.

~ Patrick Doucette

Author of:

Is Heaven for Real? Personal Stories of Visiting Heaven

http://www.amazon.com/dp/B00BXKG41U

Table of Contents

Sermon 1 - Salvation: Jesus is the Way 5

Sermon 2 - What's New? 28

Sermon 3 - Plain and Simple 47

Sermon 4 - Divine Healing..66

Sermon 5 - The Grace of God..82

Sermon 6 - The Reason Jesus Came 100

Sermon 7 - Where Is Your Treasure? 106

Sermon 8 - Notes on Giving 123

Sermon 9 - Use What God Gives...161

Sermon 10 - God's Will for Us..185

Sermon 11 - Prosperity from God 199

Sermon 12 - Prosperity Perspective..206

Afterword..218

Sermon 1 - Salvation: Jesus is the Way

In biblical times there were lots of things one could believe in...

There were all kinds of Greek or Roman 'gods' one could worship... you could take your pick! Epicureanism was a common philosophy (the teaching that pleasure was the highest good). So was Stoicism (the belief of eliminating one's emotions to reach a calm state). There were all kinds of mysterious religions and also pagan worship. There were all kinds of things one could believe in... just like there is today.

So today we're going to talk about something that is probably a very controversial topic!

First let's clarify a few things:

Most people today believe there is a God, even if they don't believe in the Christian God. Many will even go so far as to accept that Jesus is His Son, even if they don't understand what that means. Many believe there exists a Holy Spirit... they'll say "whatever—nobody understands the Spirit, anyway." They will even believe The Bible is God's Word... even though they may not believe it actually came from God, most pay lip service at least to it as a book of potential wisdom. They do not deny the reality of the church and that the church belongs to God; even if we experience it in imperfect ways.

They will NOT believe however... and THIS is where you may be called all sorts of names if you actually believe this: ...that Salvation is found in Jesus Christ... alone!

Just get ready! You're going to be called intolerant, close-minded, backwards, old-fashioned, un-enlightened, bigoted, etc!!!!

Just imagine the gall! How dare you suggest that there is only ONE way to Heaven?

There are all kinds of things one can believe in today... All kinds of religions... from Islam to Buddhism! All kinds of philosophies... from Humanism to Scientology.

It doesn't matter what you believe... we're all on the same journey; we're just taking different paths, right?

That's what our world wants to tell us...But what Peter told that panel of religious leaders in Acts 4 has never been more true! Salvation is found in no one else, for there is no other name under heaven given to men by whom we must be saved."

This great statement comes in the midst of a wonderful story in Acts.

Peter and John have been out continuing the ministry of Christ... teaching the good news and healing the sick. In chapter 3 they came across a man crippled from birth. Verse 7; Taking him by the right hand, he (Peter) helped him up, and instantly the man's feet and ankles became strong. Verse 8; He jumped to his feet and began to walk. Then he went with them into the temple courts, walking and jumping, and praising God. Verse9; When all the people saw him walking and praising God, Verse 10; they recognized him as the same man who used to sit begging at the temple gate called Beautiful, and they were filled with wonder and amazement at what had happened to him.

While the beggar held on to Peter and John, all the people were astonished and came running to them in the place called Solomon's Colonnade.

Peter knows a good opportunity when he sees it and so he starts preaching to the crowd in verse 12.

But all this preaching gets them into trouble… look down to chapter 4. The religious leaders are put out by Peter's preaching about Jesus and the resurrection and so they throw them into prison. The next day they convene a panel and drag Peter and John to appear before them. And I love what Peter says as he is "filled with the Holy Spirit" (verse 8)

Then Peter, filled with the Holy Spirit, said to them: "Rulers and elders of the people! If we are being called to account today for an act of kindness shown to a cripple and are asked how he was healed, then know this, you and all the people of Israel: It is by the name of Jesus Christ of Nazareth, whom you crucified but whom God raised from the dead, that this man stands before you healed. He is "'the stone you builders rejected, which has become the capstone.' Verse 12; Salvation is found in no one else, for there is no other name under heaven given to men by which we must be saved."

Jesus described his mission this way in Luke 19:10 "For the Son of Man came to seek and to save what was lost." Now, this was heretical teaching to the Jewish leaders! I mean, Jesus couldn't be the Messiah! The Messiah, the deliverer, the savior, was supposed to come and restore Israel's power and might… not die on a cross!

Jesus hadn't brought "salvation" from Rome! How could he be the Messiah?

Did they understand what it meant that he came "to save what was lost?"

Indeed, what does it mean that Jesus brought "salvation?" What is it "to be saved?"

It's sort of religious language that Christians like to throw around, maybe without realizing that there might be folks who don't understand what we mean by it. We sort of take it for granted that everybody wants "to be saved." Well, maybe some people don't want "to be saved" because they don't understand what it means to be lost? Maybe they don't feel the need for Jesus in their lives because they don't feel the need to be saved...?

Things are going along pretty well for them... they've got good jobs, they're paying the bills, raising their kids, shuttling them back & forth from school to soccer practice... all the while never feeling a burden to be saved, because they don't feel like they're in any trouble.

Tell me Satan hasn't done that to us! Especially in our society in America... where our wealth & prosperity and our ethic of self-reliance has blinded us to the fact that we are lost and in need of a SAVIOR!

2 Corinthians 4:4

The god of this age has blinded the minds of unbelievers, so that they cannot see the light of the gospel of the glory of Christ, who is the image of God.

But folks, the truth of the matter is that whether we realize it or not… we are LOST!

Wasn't that the message of Romans? We are all lost and we cannot save ourselves!

We have all sinned (Ro. 3:23) and what we deserve from that sin is death (6:23) but what God offers us instead is life… "but the gift of God is eternal life in Christ Jesus our Lord." (6:23b) NIV

Now, I suspect that more people realize we're in trouble than they let on. It does seem that everybody agrees that there is something wrong with us… we're just not sure what.

Some people call it dysfunction, some bad karma or psychic voids; some attribute their problems to oppression or social ills; we all sort of intuitively know that this isn't the way things are supposed to be.

So there's everything out there in the supermarket of ideas to help remedy the situation. I get sick, I go to the doctor and take a pill. I'm too fat—go to weight watchers. I suffer from addiction... alcoholism—go to alcoholics anonymous. I'm one of the millions affected by depression—there are medications I can take, counselors I can see.

There are all kinds of things out there offering us help... offering us a remedy for what ails us and I don't want to be like Tom Cruise and put any of them down... but I'll tell you that NONE of them will even come close to treating our real problem. Like a lot of things, they will only treat the symptoms... but not the root of the problem!

Our real problem... our real disease is SIN.

SIN is one of those 3-letter words that's not extremely "Politically Correct" to talk about today. We're more at home talking about diseases and dysfunction... but the heart of it all is SIN. There are two types of sin we need to consider:

One, personal sins. These are the sins that you and I commit ourselves on a sometimes daily basis. It means to "miss the mark". There are days when I sure miss it! Its these sins that we need forgiveness for.

But perhaps more profound is corporate sin. This is the sin

that is so much a part of our world, that we hardly know of anything else. We live in a fallen world and sin is all around us. It is the air we breathe in a sense… the water in which we swim. It is this sin that Paul says "entered into the world through the one man" when Adam took that fruit (Ro. 5:12). It is this sin that clouds our judgment, twists our motives and distorts our relationships. It is this sin that we cannot escape because it affects us all so profoundly. It's this sin that we need salvation from, so desperately!

Why would anyone NOT want it; salvation?

A plague was ravaging a tiny village in the outermost bush of a remote African province. A lone missionary, a doctor who had given his life to fighting this particular disease, had gone in with the only cure available. It was made from plants indigenous to the region and could quite easily be reproduced by the villagers themselves just by taking some of the leaves and mixing it with some herbs & spices. When he went in, he found that there wasn't a single person in the village who was free of the disease. They all had it and were dying at an alarming rate. Characteristic of the disease was a rash on the back of the neck. All he had to do was treat the rash with the medication and the people could be healed... but he couldn't get anybody to let him give them the medication. Despite the fact that people were dying... nobody realized that they were sick. They all had the same rash. There wasn't anything unusual about it. Since everybody had the same markings on their necks, they just assumed it was normal and nobody realized any different. Nobody realized it was killing them.

Isn't that the way it is here? We look around at the world and think this is normal. This is just the way it is, right? And nobody realizes that we're all infected by sin and it is killing us!

Folks, we are all infected and there is only one cure… Jesus Christ! He has come into our village with the only cure available… and he's the only one not sick!

It is amazing to me that even though God knew we were going to sin when he created us… he made a plan to save us, anyway.

God's plan for salvation from the very beginning was Jesus Christ!

20 He was chosen before the creation of the world, but was revealed in these last times for your sake. 1 Peter 1:20 NIV ... Sounds like a plan!

And his plan from the very beginning was for us to become his.

Ephesians 1:4-11

4 For he chose us in him before the creation of the world to be holy and blameless in his sight. In love 5 he predestined us to be adopted as his sons through Jesus Christ, ...11 In him we were also chosen, having been predestined according to the plan of him who works out everything in conformity with the purpose of his will, NIV ... Sounds like a plan!

We typically use the term "plan of salvation" in terms of

what I do… our response to the good news of Jesus. Hear the message; Believe it to be true; Confess him as Lord; Repent of our sins; Baptized into Christ--- YES, those are all things I must do!

But it is important for us to understand that those things are my response to God's plan… God's "plan of salvation" is and has always been Jesus Christ!

My sin created a wall between myself and God that I could do nothing about… until by God's plan a way was made. Jesus was made that "atoning sacrifice" (1 John 4:10) that takes away my sin… and that barrier is removed.

So I think more properly understood, the "plan of salvation" is Jesus Christ. Yet, we must still ask, "What am I you going to do about it?"

Now, if Salvation is found in Jesus ALONE...

You're not going to find it in any other religion... no matter how peaceful Moslems want you to believe Islam is, Mohammed cannot offer you true peace.

You're not going to find it in the secular world. Hope for mankind does not lie within the realm of science or technology or politics.

You're not going to find it by working harder or by trying to earn it yourself! Remember, Romans was very clear on this point. You cannot get there on your own!

Ephesians 2:8

For it is by grace you have been saved, through faith-and this not from yourselves, it is the gift of God not by works, so that no one can boast.

Salvation is a GIFT; you cannot earn it! It just doesn't work that way.

You will find it ONLY in Jesus Christ.

But... back to Acts 4 before we close... notice what Peter & John go on to do after their inquisition before the authorities.

13 When they saw the courage of Peter and John and realized that they were unschooled, ordinary men, they were astonished and they took note that these men had been with Jesus. 14 But since they could see the man who had been healed standing there with them, there was nothing they could say. 15 So they ordered them to withdraw from the Sanhedrin and then conferred together. 16 "What are we going to do with these men?"

they asked. "Everybody living in Jerusalem knows they have done an outstanding miracle, and we cannot deny it. 17 But to stop this thing from spreading any further among the people, we must warn these men to speak no longer to anyone in this name."

18 Then they called them in again and commanded them not to speak or teach at all in the name of Jesus. 19 But Peter and John replied, "Judge for yourselves whether it is right in God's sight to obey you rather than God. 20 For we cannot help speaking about what we have seen and heard."

21 After further threats they let them go. They could not decide how to punish them, because all the people were praising God for what had happened. NIV

Peter & John were so changed by their salvation in Christ

that they couldn't help from going about telling others about that good news!

They couldn't help from making a difference in the lives of people everywhere they went!

God does not simply save us from our sins (as if that was it)... He saves us FOR a purpose! Paul says in Ephesians 2:9-10

For we are God's workmanship, created in Christ Jesus to do good works, which God prepared in advance for us to do.

Part of this "plan for salvation" includes good works that he has planned for us to do!

I'm afraid many of have sort of an "ego-centric" view of salvation. That what Jesus did on the cross was JUST so I could go to Heaven... settle into that big ol' mansion on the hilltop, take daily strolls down the streets of gold, maybe a dip in the crystal sea every now and then.

Now, all of that may be true, and don't get me wrong- I'm looking forward to Heaven... but isn't that kind of an "ego-centric", selfish kind of view of salvation and Heaven itself?

Folks, Jesus didn't die JUST so you and I could live large in Heaven... but also so that we might live our lives to the glory of God right here and right now... in the midst even of all of this sin.

I mentioned Eph 1 earlier... in vss.11-12 Paul writes that we were chosen in Christ 12 in order that we, who were the first to hope in Christ, might be for the praise of his glory. NIV

We are to live our lives to the praise of God's glory! Our lives should be shining examples in a dark world of the light of Christ!

Salvation is found in Jesus Christ… He is the way!

The question for us may not be "Are you saved?" …though I need to ask you that this morning. Particularly to our young people who may be thinking about what they are going to give their lives to.

Have you given your life to Jesus Christ? Have you accepted God's plan of Salvation and given your life to Jesus?

Do you believe that He is the Son of God? Have you confessed His name as Lord of your life? Have you turned from your sin and made a decision to follow Him? Have your sins been washed away in the waters of baptism? Are you a Christian?

Most of us have... probably a long time ago. Maybe the question you ought to consider this morning is, "How is my salvation reaching others?"

Has it at all? Are you telling others about Jesus?

Are you living your life to bring glory to God?

Is your salvation being demonstrated by your works and your actions?

Have you found salvation this morning? It's in Jesus! Accept Him today and pray with me...

Sermon 2 - What's New?

People are craving for new things today more than ever.

New phones, new cars, new clothes, new hairstyles, and even a new face.

People go for plastic surgery to get a new nose, new ears, a new look, new body…

Especially during New Year, we want to set new goals, new resolutions

For the Chinese, during Chinese New Year, we wear new clothes, new shoes…

New furniture for the home… If we can change

everything, we would.

Anything that is external, that is. That's what we can change. And it's simple.

But we cannot CHANGE us – the real me! I can change my clothes but it's still me.

You might see me with a new hairdo, but it would still be me.

I carry with me the same old handicaps, worries, fears... same sadness and miseries.

No amount of new gadgets, clothes or things can really give me what my heart longs for.

WHY? Because what we need are not new things, but a new life.

We can have many new things but we cannot have a new life, unless we come to Christ.

The Bible says only in Jesus Christ can we have a NEW LIFE — a new creation.

It's not an EXTERNAL change — I still look the same. It is internal.

I experience God's love, joy, peace, and hope. These inspire me and change me.

Man cannot see these things. The man who looks handsome on the outside may be a miserable man. The one who looks shabby may be one of the happiest men around.

So before we are too drawn away by the sights and

sounds of this world, tell yourself – "I need to hang on to Jesus." Do you want to be really happy in life, try getting to know Jesus more.

Listen to Jesus - John 10:10 "I have come that they may have life, and have it to the full."

I am already living, why give me life? Obviously it not about just living - we can be living without a life, without meaning and purpose, you can be alive but not know what you are living for.

Jesus refers to an abundant life, a full life. In John 17:3 He says, "Now this is eternal life: that they may know you, the only true God, and Jesus Christ, whom you have sent."

Man has made great improvements over the Centuries. The speed at which we are gaining knowledge is amazing.

Half of all that we learn in the history of mankind was acquired in the last 10 years! We have made great strides in education, science, technology – the new gadgets we have.

Yet life has not been better. Life is made easy but not better.

We live with the same worries and fears, probably MORE. We worry about not having enough; we fear being diagnosed with cancer of some kind; we have relationship problems – at school, at home, at work, even among close friends. We have more broken families today, a growing number of suicides and divorces today than ever. And we see more violence. We need to have anti-terrorism drills. Life has not improved. Why? Because man has fallen away from God.

So if you really want a good life – get back to Jesus. Talk to Him, and keep talking to Him.

Jesus will make you NEW.

It's like an old house – He did not renovate it, He rebuilt it. Jesus describes in John 2:19, "Destroy this temple, and I will raise it again in three days." The life we have in Christ is an entirely NEW creation.

It's like the story of a man who was selling an old warehouse. The building had been empty for months and needed repairs. Gangs had damaged the doors, smashed the windows, and thrown trash everywhere.

As he showed a prospective buyer the property, he took

pains to say that he would replace the broken windows, bring in a crew to correct any structural damage, and clean out the garbage.

The buyer smiled and said, "Forget about the repairs. When I buy this place, I'm going to build something completely different. I don't want the building; I want the site."

Jesus puts it this way to Nicodemus, "you must be born again." (John 3:3)

Let me tell you the story of a simple, illiterate man who was converted through the work of the Salvation Army. He went regularly to the Salvation Army citadel. One day he came home rather upset.

His wife said, "What's the matter?"

He said, "I've just noticed that all the people in the Salvation Army wear red sweaters, and I don't have a red sweater."

She said, "I'll knit one for you." So she knitted him a red sweater.

The next Sunday after he went to the citadel, he still wasn't happy.

His wife said, "What's wrong this time?"

He said, "I just noticed all their red sweaters have yellow writing."

They were both illiterate, but she said, "Don't worry about it. I'll embroider some writing on it for you." She had no idea what the yellow writing on the red sweater of a Salvation Army man said - Any of you know what it is? The man's wife had no idea what the letters said, and she couldn't read anyway. So copying a sign from a store window opposite their home, she embroidered the words of that store sign onto his red sweater.

When he came back the next Sunday, she said, "Did they like your sweater?"

"They loved my sweater. Some of them smiled at me when they saw my sweater."

What neither of them knew was that the sign on the store window she had copied read, UNDER NEW MANAGEMENT.

We don't really need better gadgets, better things, or better programs. We need to come under new management, we need JESUS.

Let's make this one of your resolutions this year – get to know Him better. Spend time with Him.

Heb 10:25 says "Let us not give up meeting together, as some are in the habit of doing, but let us encourage one another-and all the more as you see the Day approaching."

It's not because God is lonely. It is for our sake. We need to stay close to God.

Don't neglect your fellowship meetings. Some people call them Yum and Yam meetings. Social groups are good but they can replace church groups, because there is something here that they do not have. You see, the issue is not about friendship, having a good time chatting, eating or having fun.

It's about nurturing this NEW LIFE – and only in church can we find this. Outside, you can only nurture your OLD LIFE – which is to eat, sleep and be merry. And then you die.

Don't look for peace in this world – if you are, you are looking in the wrong place.

We have joy, because the Lord is with us, not because our circumstance is good.

We have peace, because the Lord lives in my heart, not because there is no trouble.

We have hope, because the Lord guides us, not because of our wisdom and strength.

We want to remind ourselves to stay close to God, and

encourage one another to do so.

Verse 19b-20: And he has committed to us the message of reconciliation. 20 We are therefore Christ's ambassadors, as though God were making his appeal through us.

Not only do we have a new life, we have a new purpose.

Every January people talk about making resolutions for the new year.

Some say they will exercise more, stop smoking, eat healthy, and make more friends...

These are good; but they are just temporary goals.

As Christians, we have a lifetime goal. This is a resolution for life!

The world must know. And now we must tell them.

See it this way:

In many areas people often battle floods when the rivers overflow, we see people filling up sandbags with sand and stacking them up to prevent waters from entering a village or town.

If you know that you're going to save the town, you're going to work with all your might. There is nothing glamorous about filling bags with sand, but saving the town is something else altogether. You have an honorable goal.

If you would to ask people to do that where there are no rivers, nobody is going to do it. It's meaningless.

A man came to a construction site, where stonemasons were working. The man said to one, "What are you doing?"

The stonemason said, "You can see, I'm chipping a stone."

The man walked over to another mason and said, "What are you doing?"

He answered, "I'm building a wall."

The man walked over to a third mason and said, "What are you doing?"

This mason answered, "I am building a church."

All three were doing the same thing, but what a

difference perspective makes!

Day in day out, what are you living for - three meals a day? Or eat, work and sleep?

We have a God-given purpose! We have to see everything in that light.

It does not mean we have to be preachy all the time. We have to cultivate a concern for the welfare of the souls of others!

A young man, a skilled mechanic, was driving a visiting pastor from his home town, 50 miles across the country, to another city. En route, they passed a huge factory consisting of perhaps 20 buildings scattered over several hundred acres.

"Do you see that red brick building over there behind this grey stone one?" the mechanic asked. "I work on the second floor on the south side. There are 74 of us in that department, and as far as I know, I am the only one in all that crowd who ever goes to church or tries to live a Christian life.

Sometimes I have to remind myself that, as far as that department is concerned, I am all there is of the Christian church. If I don't do good work, then the church has failed as far as those men are concerned. If I can't be relied upon, then the church is undependable. If I am careless, then some poor unfortunate soul may have to pay for the church's carelessness.

It is pretty serious business being the church in the midst

of 74 other people."

'What does Christ's ambassador do?' you ask. He...

(a) knows the heart of Christ

(b) stays in constant communication with Christ

(c) keeps his heart set on Christ's interests alone

(d) in this world represents Christ well

(e) is ready for recall at a moment's notice.

We are betraying His trust if we live only for the here and now, and only for ourselves.

C. S. Lewis says, "All that is not eternal is eternally useless."

What are you living for?

Every year, during the New Year, we wish that everything will be new and good.

We've already pass so many New Year, are we better off today?

What we need – cannot be found in this world. We need a new life, because we're in sin.

We need a Savior in Jesus Christ.

Dear friends, the Bible says, you need to be reconciled with God, your Creator.

The man who is in Christ will experience newness of life!

You need to put your trust in Jesus. You need to rely upon Him.

People have been trying - by their own efforts - to do right and live right.

But the Bible says we've all sinned and fallen short of God's glory.

By our own efforts, we can never be good enough.

No amount of change can truly improve our lives.

No amount of education can give us a good life. We need a change of heart.

We need the forgiveness of our sins. We need a new life.

Only Jesus Christ can do that. Believe in Him today.

Sermon 3 - Plain and Simple

Pastor H.A. Ironside of Moody Church in Chicago tells a story of how one day he rode a passenger train and a gypsy woman sat down beside him, and said, "sir, if you cross my palm with some silver, I'll tell you your future! Pastor Ironside said, "before you do that, let me show you what God says about my future..." He proceeded to open the Bible. She said, 'that's ok, I've had quite enough". He stopped her and said "no, I want you to see this: in the past there is guilt; in the present there is grace; and in the future there is glory! The gypsy woman ran away down the train crying out, I picked the wrong man!

You can call Madame Fortune Teller; The Crystal Ball Reader or even the Psychic Friends Network but they can't help you. When it comes to my future, I prefer the Word of God!

Salvation exists in the past, present, and future.

Being "saved" is not a Baptist thing; it's not a Pentecostal thing…it's not a term we've made up…it's a Bible term!

No other Name given under heaven among men whereby we must be _____ (saved!)

Whosoever shall call upon the Name of the Lord shall be _____(saved!)

Have you been saved? How do you know? Put it into words...what's the answer (is it predominantly I or predominantly God?)

Salvation is of the Lord...too many people are trying to save themselves. They're trying to earn it; they're trying to be good enough; they're basically trying to save themselves! It's not about us...it's about God!

Two of the most precious words in scripture are: "but God"

Ps 49:15 -

But God will redeem my soul from the power of the grave: for he shall receive me. Selah.

Matthew 2:7 - ... who can forgive sins **but God** only?

Lu 16:15 -

And he said unto them, Ye are they which justify yourselves before men; **but God** knoweth your hearts: for that which is highly esteemed among men is abomination in the sight of God.

Romans 5:8 -

But God commendeth his love toward us, in that, while we were yet sinners, Christ died for us.

1Corinthians 3:6 -

I have planted, Apollos watered; **but God** gave the increase.

So then neither is he that planteth any thing, neither he that watereth; **but God** that giveth the increase.

Eph 2:4 -

But God, who is rich in mercy, for his great love

wherewith he loved us…

It doesn't say "but you", it says, "but God!"

In the garden of Eden, Adam and Eve sinned. They lost their innocence, realized they were naked and tried to cover it with fig leaves. It is really a picture of people trying to cover their own sinfulness. But God came along and shed the blood of an innocent animal and clothed them with the skin. This is the first demonstration of blood being shed for sin. The innocent dying for the guilty.

Are you trying to cover yourself? You cannot do it. Our righteousness is as filthy rags.

Are you wearing fig leaves?

Fig leaves of Baptism, confirmation, church attendance,

offerings, good works, keeping the Ten Commandments and on and on…?

"but I'm a good person"… "no, but God"

Not but baptism….no, but God"

Salvation is of the Lord…you cannot save yourself

You may as well try to blow back a tornado with an electric fan or dam up Niagara falls with toothpicks, it just ain't gonna work!

1. Who Saves? God alone!

2. Why does God save us?

Because of love and mercy!

Hard to understand the depths of His love!

(it may be easy to love someone who's lovable/loving/lovely...but God loved us while we were yet sinners!)

May not understand it, but let's thank God for it!

P.P. Bliss wrote many hymns including "O How I Love Jesus"... "because He first loved me"

he wrote this at a young age, later in life he wrote:

I am so glad that my Father in Heaven tells of His love in the book He has given. Now that was a man who was impressed with God's love!

A great theologian was teaching at a seminary and students came to him and said, we'd like to know the most profound truth that's ever occupied your mind? (expecting some deep doctrine) and he said, it was on my mother's knee as she sang: Jesus loves me this I know…!

Why does God save us? Because of Love!
Why does God love us? I don't know!

Also because of His mercy.
Mercy is not receiving the punishment you rightfully deserve!

A lady went to the photographer for a portrait; "do me justice she pleaded!" The photographer replied, "you need mercy!"

Mercy is not receiving the punishment you rightfully deserve!

What is it that we rightfully deserve?

Death and hell!...if you only committed one sin, God could not allow you into heaven! We're all painfully aware of what sinners we are! Some don't believe they CAN be saved from all they've done:

    A poor woman from slums of London/taken on holiday by friends to the ocean/arrived...just gazed out...started crying/they wondered why on such a nice day/she said, "it's the first thing I've ever seen that there's enough of!"

There's enough mercy in God's little finger to wipe away

every sin you've ever committed!

Who saves? God alone!

Why? Love and Mercy

How does God save?

Grace (not by love "I believe in a God of love that would never send anyone to hell"...Jn. 3:16—God so loved that he saved or gave [then we have to choose])

It's the opposite of mercy...grace is receiving something good that you don't deserve

GRACE=God's Redemption at Christ's Expense

What does God give us that we don't deserve?

Heaven (yes, but what now that makes it possible?)

The righteousness of Christ!

We're not only saved FROM something but TO something...not only are we saved from sin (forgiven), but we become the recipients of Christ's righteousness!...clothed in His righteousness!! (imputed righteousness ["I don't live very righteous sometimes"...not imparted—that's sanctification] Positional righteousness [justification...a legal standing)

God looks at the saved, born-again Christian and sees: not just a forgiven sinner, but a justified one [just as if I'd never sinned!] That's Grace!

Who saves? God alone!

Why? Love and Mercy

How does God save? By Grace!

When does God Save?

When true Biblical faith occurs

Notice it doesn't say we are saved BY faith, but THRU faith...we're saved by Grace, and Faith is the vehicle that gets us there!

FAITH=Forsaking All I Trust Him

Too many people have missed salvation because they trust in Christ + something else...true Biblical faith is Jesus Christ + nothing – nothing.

For example if I place one leg on the pew, am I trusting it to hold me up? No, part of my faith is in the pew but part is in the floor! It is similar to one trusting Christ plus themselves, plus baptism, plus good works, you get the idea.

True Biblical Faith is Christ alone... Forsaking All I Trust Him

Don't think you'll make it there on your own

Not How Great I Am, but How Great Thou Art!

You have to trust in Jesus alone and His death in your place, His blood in your stead!

In and of yourself, you cannot make it to heaven...realize you NEED to be saved/CAN be saved only because of Jesus!

Who saves? God alone!

Why? Love and Mercy

How does God save? By Grace!

When does God Save?

When true Biblical faith occurs

Where does that leave us?

I'm not the smartest in the world, but not the dumbest either! "has raised" … is that future or has it already taken place?

If I'm saved, then in the mind of God, I'm as sure of heaven as if I'd already been there a million years!

Eph. 1:3 (read)

We're already there! "do you know you're going to heaven" most say, "I hope so"…well, if you're saved, you're already there!

That's good to know, because it means I can view every circumstance of life from a heavenly perspective.

"How you doin'?"... "well, good, under the circumstances" God doesn't want us to live under there! He wants us to view it all from a higher perspective!! What does it matter next to eternity?

Your salvation has a present tense...you might have hard circumstances...but God...!/down in the dumps but you're in the heavenlies/may think you're pretty low/it may appear Satan has you by the throat sometimes...but God has you somewhere else!...in the heavenlies!

Genesis 31:7 -

And your father hath deceived me, and changed my wages ten times; but God suffered him not to hurt me.

Genesis 48:21 -

And Israel said unto Joseph, Behold, I die: but God shall be with you...

Genesis 50:20 -

But as for you, ye thought evil against me; but God meant it unto good...

1Samuel 23:14 -

And David abode in the wilderness in strong holds, and remained in a mountain in the wilderness of Ziph. And Saul sought him every day, but God delivered him not into his hand.

2 Chronicles 20:15 -

And he said, Hearken ye, all Judah, and ye inhabitants of Jerusalem, and thou king Jehoshaphat, Thus saith the

LORD unto you, Be not afraid nor dismayed by reason of this great multitude; for the battle is not yours, but God's.

Psalm 64:7 -

But God shall shoot at them with an arrow; suddenly shall they be wounded.

Psalm 73:26 -

My flesh and my heart faileth: but God is the strength of my heart, and my portion for ever.

1Corinthians 10:13 -

There hath no temptation taken you but such as is common to man: but God is faithful, who will not suffer you to be tempted above that ye are able; but will with the temptation also make a way to escape, that ye may be able to bear it.

Philippians 2:27 -

For indeed he was sick nigh unto death: but God had mercy on him; and not on him only, but on me also, lest I should have sorrow upon sorrow.

Who saves? God alone!

Why? Love and Mercy

How does God save? By Grace!

When does God Save?

When true Biblical faith occurs

Where does that leave us? In heavenly places!

Lord, thank you for the simplicity of salvation...

You cannot face God someday w/ anything less than Jesus

as your Savior...you cannot save yourself...no ifs, ands, or buts... "but God!" Pray with me today...

Sermon 4 - Divine Healing

My desire in this sermon is to show from the Scriptures that God is both able and willing to heal the sick, the diseased and the infirm. Let's turn now to the Bible to see its revelation of this great truth of spiritual healing.

- **Sick believers don't need to remain sick!**

James 5:14 Is any one of you sick? He should call the <u>elders</u> of the church to pray over him..."James was writing to Christian believers (2:1). He asked them if any of them were sick. It is a "given" of life in our fallen condition that our bodies on occasion do get sick; and eventually they die. However, as the verse directly below points out, it is also a "given" for the believer that God is Jehovah-Rapha, "the Lord who heals you."

Exodus 15:26 [God] said, "If you listen carefully to the voice of the LORD your God and do what is right in his eyes, if you pay attention to his commands and keep all his decrees, I will not bring on you any of the diseases I brought on the Egyptians, for I am the LORD, who heals you." God identified Himself to Israel in a variety of names and ways. Here He revealed Himself to His people as "Jehovah-Rapha" — "the Lord who heals you."

Healing is not just something that God "does." No, it's more than that, healing is part of God's very nature — "I AM the Lord who heals you." Remember always that you serve a healing God who has declared that His intent towards you is "not to bring on you any diseases ... but to be the Lord who heals you."

• **God is FOR us, not against us, in the matter of healing.**

God's heart towards His people is health and healing. See, for example, the following Scripture portions: Exodus 23:25-26 Worship the LORD your God, and his blessing will be on your food and water. I will take away sickness from among you, and none will miscarry or be barren in your land. I will give you a full life span. Deuteronomy 7:11-12, 15 Therefore, take care to follow the commands, decrees and laws I give you today. If you pay attention to these laws and are careful to follow them, then the LORD your God will keep his covenant of love with you, as he swore to your forefathers.... [15] The LORD will keep you free from every disease. He will not inflict on you the horrible diseases you knew in Egypt, but he will inflict them on all who hate you.

Acts 10:38 ...how God anointed Jesus of Nazareth with the Holy Spirit and power, and how he went around doing good and healing all who were under the power of the devil, because God was with him.

- **God's spiritual healing power extends to ALL our diseases and infirmities.**

Psalms 103:2-3 Praise the LORD, O my soul, and forget not all his benefits — who forgives all your sins and heals all your diseases. The greatest of the Lord's "benefits" is that He forgives all our sins! But the Psalmist here charges us not to forget another of the Lord's benefits — that is, He "heals all our diseases." ALL our diseases! None are too hard for Him. No illnesses are excluded from this great "benefit." Whatever disease you or a loved one may have, it falls under God's promise to "heal all your diseases."

- **Jesus died for both our sins and our sicknesses.**

Isaiah 53:5 But he was pierced for our transgressions, he was crushed for our iniquities; the punishment that brought us peace was upon him, and by his wounds we are healed.

1 Peter 2:24 He himself bore our sins in his body on the tree, so that we might die to sins and live for righteousness; by his wounds you have been healed.

It was Jesus' willing offering of Himself on the Cross that bore our sins. But the very same tormented body of Jesus, in His scourging and crucifixion, purchased for us the blessing of divine healing — "by His wounds you have been healed."

And notice the differences in the verb tenses used by Isaiah and Peter. Isaiah, prophetically seeing this seven centuries before Christ, said, "By His wounds we are healed." The apostle Peter, looking back to Christ's historical death and resurrection, declared, "By His wounds you have been healed." Jesus cried out from the Cross, "It is finished!" Sin has been overcome. Sickness has been overcome. The Cross of Jesus Christ has conquered both sin and sickness. The following are some of the numerous instances of divine, spiritual healing in the Bible. Let's see what insights we can learn from them.

- **God responds to prayer for healing.**

Genesis 20:17-18 Then Abraham prayed to God, and God healed Abimelech, his wife and his slave girls so they could have children again, for the LORD had closed up every womb in Abimelech's household because of Abraham's wife Sarah.

Numbers 12:13 So Moses cried out to the LORD, "O God, please heal her!"

The principle here is simple — faithful Abraham prayed, and God healed. Moses prayed for leprous Miriam, and God healed her. King David understood the power of prayer for healing the sick — "O LORD my God, I called to you for help and you healed me" (Psalm 30:2).

The ongoing principle seen here and elsewhere in the Bible, is the power of a believer's prayer. Abraham, Moses, and David believed in God's healing power and His willingness to heal, and they prayed for it. Jesus taught on this same power of a believer's faith-filled prayer:

Matthew 21:22 "If you believe, you will receive whatever you ask for in prayer."

- **And it's OK with God if our prayers for healing are deeply emotional!**

2 Kings 20:1-5 (King James Version) In those days was Hezekiah sick unto death. And the prophet Isaiah the son of Amoz came to him, and said unto him, Thus saith the LORD, Set thine house in order; for thou shalt die, and not live. Then he turned his face to the wall, and prayed unto the LORD, saying, I beseech thee, O LORD, remember now how I have walked before thee in truth and with a perfect heart, and have done that which is good in thy sight. And Hezekiah wept sore. And it came to pass, afore Isaiah was gone out into the middle court, that the word of the LORD came to him, saying, Turn again, and tell Hezekiah the captain of my people, Thus saith the LORD, the God of David thy father, I have heard thy prayer, I have seen thy tears: behold, I will heal thee: on the third day thou shalt go up unto the house of the LORD.

Serious illnesses can be emotionally devastating. King Hezekiah was "sick unto death." To make matters worse, the prophet Isaiah brought him the Lord's message that this illness would be fatal. Hezekiah's reaction is very illuminating for us.

The Bible reveals to us that, having learned that his illness was terminal, Hezekiah "wept bitterly" as he "prayed unto the Lord." Note that God regarded both Hezekiah's prayer and his emotions — "I have heard thy prayer; I have seen thy tears: behold, I will heal thee." It's OK with God if we are quite emotional in approaching Him with our healing needs.

Now let's look at some examples of Jesus healing the sick, the infirm, the diseased, those in pain, etc.

• Jesus healed a broad range of illnesses — in fact, He healed "every disease and sickness."

Matthew 4:23-24 Jesus went throughout Galilee, teaching in their synagogues, preaching the good news of the kingdom, and HEALING EVERY disease and sickness among the people. News about him spread all over Syria, and people brought to him all who were ill with various diseases, those suffering severe pain, the demon-possessed, those having seizures, and the paralyzed, and he healed them.

Christians serve a healing Savior, Jesus Christ. His heart, as here, is for "the people." The Gospel records abound with illustrations of Jesus healing the masses, the men and women on the street. He preached and taught, yes. But He also "healed every disease and sickness among the people."

"Every disease and sickness" — Christ's healing power is without limit. His healing touch is available to everyone. There is no illness beyond His ability to cure. He healed them all, so don't hesitate to bring any healing need to Jesus, because He demonstrated His ability and His willingness to heal "**every** disease and sickness among the people."

- **BELIEVE the Lord for divine healing. Have FAITH in His power and willingness to heal you.**

Matthew 9:20-22, 27-30a (KJV) And, behold, a woman, which was diseased with an issue of blood twelve years, came behind him, and touched the hem of his garment: For she said within herself, If I may but touch his garment, I shall be whole. But Jesus turned him about, and when he saw her, he said, Daughter, be of good comfort; thy faith hath made thee whole. And the woman was made whole from that hour.... [27] And when Jesus departed thence, two blind men followed him, crying, and saying, Thou Son of David, have mercy on us. And when he was come into the house, the blind men came to him: and Jesus saith unto them, Believe ye that I am able to do this? They said unto him, Yea, Lord. Then touched he their eyes, saying, According to your faith be it unto you. And their eyes were opened.

A principle of great importance is seen in these verses — that is, "thy faith hath made thee whole ... according to your faith be it unto you." Hebrews 11:6 tells us that "without faith it is impossible to please God." But conversely, we are told, "If you believe, you will receive whatever you ask for in prayer" (Matthew 21:22). God expects us, in asking for healing as well as in other prayers, to believe Him, to believe His word, to "have faith in God" (Mark 11:22). Divine healing is quite appropriately called "faith healing"!

- **God may ask us to demonstrate our faith for spiritual healing.**

Matthew 12:10, 13 And a man with a shriveled hand was there. Looking for a reason to accuse Jesus, they asked him, "Is it lawful to heal on the Sabbath?" ... [13] Then he said to the man, "Stretch out your hand." So he stretched it out and it was completely restored, just as sound as the other.

There may be times when the Lord will ask you to show your faith, to give observable evidence of your faith, as in the case of the man whom He told to stretch out his withered hand.

- **Healing comes through faith in Jesus, not faith in faith.**

Acts 3:16 By faith in the name of JESUS, this man whom you see and know was made strong. It is JESUS' name and the faith that comes through HIM that has given this complete healing to him, as you can all see.

Healing comes "by faith in" someone — JESUS! Over the years I have heard sincere Christians misdirect their faith. Some have fallen into the error of having "faith in faith." No! Our faith is in a Person, Jesus, who heals. Others have properly searched the Scriptures concerning healing, but have unfortunately been content to use them merely as a "formula" for healing, rather than as a revelation of the Healer Himself. "Faith healing" is not primarily believing the doctrine of healing (true as that doctrine is), but believing in the Healer, the Person — that is, in Jesus Christ.

Peter understood the proper object of our faith — Jesus! He told his listeners how the lame man had been healed:

- "...by faith in the name of Jesus"

- "It is Jesus' name..."

- "It is...the faith that comes through Him..."

• Sometimes we may need to "walk" for a while in faith, then the healing comes.

Luke 17:12 And as he entered into a certain village, there met him ten men that were lepers, which stood afar off: And they lifted up their voices, and said, Jesus,

Master, have mercy on us. And when he saw them, he said unto them, Go shew yourselves unto the priests. And it came to pass, that, as they went, they were cleansed.

This is a very reassuring verse. Notice that the lepers were not healed the moment they prayed. No, but rather they were healed "as they went" to show themselves to the priests in obedience to Jesus.

There may be times when we need to "walk" for a while in faith, and then the healing comes. Although many healings in the Bible were instantaneous, some were not immediate. Be willing to maintain steadfast faith as you pray for divine healing, and don't be discouraged if your healing does not immediately occur.

- **Don't pray, then doubt!**

In his epistle James reveals a valuable principle for the person asking something of God "When he asks, he must believe and not doubt, because he who doubts is like a wave of the sea, blown and tossed by the wind. That man should not think he will receive anything from the Lord" (James 1:6-7). When you ask God for healing, don't doubt! Don't waver! Believe God. Believe the healing promises of His word. Reject doubt, choosing rather to say, "God is true ... His word is true ... so my doubts must go!"

- Now let us look at seven ways HOW healing is ministered to people.

1. By prayer, as we have already seen.

2. By a spoken word.

John 4:49-51 The nobleman saith unto him, Sir, come down ere my child die. Jesus saith unto him, Go thy way; thy son liveth. And the man believed the word that Jesus had spoken unto him, and he went his way. And as he was now going down, his servants met him, and told him, saying, Thy son liveth.

Even at a distance from the nobleman's home, Jesus spoke the word: "Thy son liveth." And the man "believed the word that Jesus had spoken" and returned home to find his son alive. There is healing power in the spoken word of faith.

Acts 9:33-34 There he found a man named Aeneas, a paralytic who had been bedridden for eight years. "Aeneas," Peter said to him, "Jesus Christ heals you. Get up and take care of your mat." Immediately Aeneas got up.

Again, we see the power of the spoken word of faith. Peter simply declared the truth: "Jesus Christ heals you." Tell the sick, "Jesus Christ heals you." Make no apologies for that statement. Don't doubt it. Don't try to water it down. As the old saying goes, truer words were never spoken!

Acts 14:8-10, KJV And there sat a certain man at Lystra, impotent in his feet, being a cripple from his mother's womb, who never had walked: The same heard Paul speak: who stedfastly beholding him, and perceiving that he had faith to be healed, said with a loud voice, Stand upright on thy feet. And he leaped and walked.

Once more we see the healing power of the spoken word of faith. The preaching of the word of God inspired an atmosphere of faith. Paul "perceived that [the lame man] had faith to be healed."

How did the lame man come to this place of having faith to be healed? The answer is that he heard the word of God spoken by Paul. This is a vitally important principle for all churches and all Christians. Preach the word. Teach the word. God's word will inspire faith in the hearers. And we will begin to see dramatic healings in response to the spoken word of faith — "Stand upright on thy feet!"

3. By the laying on of hands.

Acts 9:10-11, 17-18, KJV And there was a certain disciple at Damascus, named Ananias; and to him said the Lord in a vision, Ananias. And he said, Behold, I am here, Lord. And the Lord said unto him, Arise, and go into the street which is called Straight, and enquire in the house of Judas for one called Saul, of Tarsus.... [17] And Ananias went his way, and entered into the house; and putting his hands on him said, Brother Saul, the Lord, even Jesus, that appeared unto thee in the way as thou camest, hath sent me, that thou mightest receive thy sight, and be filled with the Holy Ghost. And immediately there fell from his eyes as it had been scales: and he received sight forthwith, and arose, and was baptized.

First notice that it doesn't require an apostle to heal the sick. It doesn't require someone with a special healing ministry to heal the sick. Verse 10 identifies Ananias simply as a "disciple." Mark 16:17-18 records Jesus' promise to all believers — "And these signs will accompany those who believe.... they will place their hands on sick people, and they will get well."

Led by Jesus in a vision, the faithful "disciple" Ananias found Saul and announced that Jesus had sent him to heal Saul's blindness. It is important for those who are sick to understand that Jesus is able and willing to heal them.

Then Ananias laid his hands on him, and Saul's eyes immediately received sight again.

4. By filling the needy person's heart with the faith-building, life-giving word of God.

Proverbs 4:20-22 My son, pay attention to what I say; listen closely to my words. Do not let them out of your sight, keep them within your heart; for they are life to those who find them and health to a man's whole body. The words of the Lord, as recorded in the Bible, are life-giving — "they are life." Jesus said that His words "are spirit and they are life."

But the Proverb reveals another dramatic benefit of keeping the Lord's words "within your heart," and that benefit is health — "My words ...[are] health to a man's whole body." The secular world speaks of "alternative health". But the best source of alternative health — or any aspect of health! — is the sure promises of God in His word, the bible.

5. A merry heart contributes to our receiving spiritual healing.

Proverbs 17:22 A merry heart doeth good like a medicine: but a broken spirit drieth the bones. One interpretation could be that a joyful heart "literally, 'causes good healing.' "

Think of that — the state of our "heart" — referring here to the emotions, not the bodily organ — can substantially affect our good health or lack thereof. This has long been common knowledge in the medical field. Sometimes illnesses are diagnosed as "psychosomatic" in origin. Interestingly, the word psychosomatic comes from the same Greek words that the Bible uses for "soul" and "body." So medical science agrees with the Bible that the state of our inner man or woman can substantially affect our physical health, for good or for bad.

The word of God says that a merry heart "literally causes good healing"! There is a direct, cause-and-effect result: merry heart —> good healing. Conversely, a broken or crushed spirit has a negative effect on our health (it "dries up the bones").

One of the fruits of the Spirit (Galatians 5:22) is joy. Those who allow the presence of the Lord in their lives to bring a daily, inward joy will also reap the wonderful promise of their "merry heart doing good like a medicine."

6. There is healing in "the Lord's Supper," the Communion.

1 Corinthians 11:29-30 For anyone who eats and drinks [the Lord's supper, vs. 20] without recognizing the body of the Lord eats and drinks judgment on himself. That is why many among you are weak and sick, and a number of you have fallen asleep.

"That is why many...are weak and sick." Why? They take Communion "without recognizing the body of the Lord." They forget 1 Peter 2:24 — "By his wounds you have been healed." They participate in the communion service, perhaps needing a physical healing, and remain oblivious to the fact that Jesus' body bore both our sins and our sicknesses.

I would encourage every reader to ponder these things the next time you take communion. Remember what Jesus' broken body has done for you. Receive the benefits of that by faith. And expect divine healing to come to your body, even during the very communion service.

7. By calling the elders of the church to lay on hands, anoint with oil, and pray for you.

James 5:14-15 Is any one of you sick? He should call the elders of the church to pray over him and anoint him with oil in the name of the Lord. And the prayer offered in faith will make the sick person well; the Lord will raise him up.

An important doctrinal point on a related topic — it's important for each church to have members that are recognized as elders. Otherwise, there are no "elders of the church" for the sick to call for prayer and anointing with oil. Can you identify the elders of your church?

Remember Exodus 15:26 I am the Lord, who heals you.

Psalms 103:1-3 Praise the LORD, O my soul; all my inmost being, praise his holy name. Praise the LORD, O my soul, and forget not all his benefits — who forgives all your sins and heals all your diseases. Amen.

Sermon 5 - The Grace of God

One of the most well known stories Jesus ever told begins with a bold, almost shocking request. The first hearers of this parable must have been amazed at the brashness of the Prodigal Son. The insolence of it would have been almost unimaginable for them. "Father," the youngest son said, "give me the share of property that falls to me."

The only way a son could claim his inheritance was on the death of his father. "Dad," the younger son said in effect, "I wish you were dead; I wish you were out of the way so I could start a new life on my own."

In all of Middle Eastern literature ... from ancient times to the present, there is no case of any son, older or younger, asking for his inheritance from a father who is still in good health" -- except in this parable. You could say Jesus knew how to grab the attention of His listeners!

And if they were surprised at the cruel implications of this selfish demand, they would have been blown out of their sandals by the response of the father. Any Israelite would have expected the father to explode in anger and discipline. Instead, they heard Jesus tell of a father who loved in an astonishing way, who loved enough to grant his son the freedom to reject that love, the freedom to make wrong choices, the freedom even to hurt himself in order maybe to find himself. He gave in to the son's request and the young son in turn set out for the far country.

The far country! It had seduced his imagination by day and ravished his dreams by night. His heart had long ago left home, of course, and travelled to the land of restless longing. But now he would catch up with his heart; now he would not awaken from his dream to face another dull day of drudgery in his father's fields; now he would actually live his dream.

With cold cash in his pocket and hot desire in his body, he succumbed to the centrifugal pull of pleasure; he bolted into unrestrained ecstasies of the flesh; he became a one-man stampede of self-indulgence -- trampling, mutilating, exhausting everything noble in him. As the King James version so quaintly puts it, "He wasted his substance with riotous living."

It was not a good time to blow his cash. He was generous with money when the sky was stingy with rain. Famine gripped the land, and the stranglehold brought hunger and death. The prodigal had no choice but to find work. There aren't many options in a famine; you take what you can get. You grovel, accept humiliation -- anything to survive.

So the one who greedily seized freedom had freedom turn in upon him until he was locked in a prison he could never have imagined before leaving home. The text graphically tells us that he "glued" himself to a citizen of that country. And that citizen sent him (sent this one who wanted freedom more than anything else) to do the most detestable thing imaginable for a Jew: he forced him to feed the pigs.

The degradation wasn't finished. He still wasn't making enough to stay alive. He was so hungry he found himself wishing he could eat the pig slop. Yes, he would have chewed on the bitter wild carob and like the pigs have grubbed for its berries, had he been able to get away with it. But the owner watched his every move.

"But when he came to himself," Jesus said. "What a gracious way of saying it. Jesus mercifully puts the best possible light on his crimes. "When he came to himself." In truth, when he had turned his back on his father, he had turned his back on himself. He had not been himself, not really, when he took off on a self-centered quest for pleasure. But when he came to himself, when his eyes were opened, he saw his true situation. He saw that while he was mucking about up to his knees in mud and excrement, and so hungry he would have been glad to trade places with the pigs, his father's day-laborers had more than enough bread to spare.

Swallowing his pride, at that point, was easier than swallowing death. So he decided to go home. His motives were not great. He had given no thought to his father's suffering, no thought to his own shame. It was a matter of survival. Not the best reason to go home, perhaps, but it was enough. It turned him around.

That's what repentance is -- turning toward home. Perhaps you need to do that today. Perhaps you've travelled to the far country of your own choosing, taken matters into your own hands, lusted after personal freedom and seized it the first chance you've had; you've given no thought to the Father.

But now you find yourself in the horrible poverty of meaningless affluence, or the pig pen of moral guilt, or you feel a hunger gnawing at your insides which promises death. It's time to go home.

The prodigal knew it was time for him. So he repented, in a way. It was really a weak, distorted repentance. It got him headed in the right direction, but it was filled with all the pride that got him into trouble in the first place. You see, he developed a plan. He wanted to retain some dignity, have some control over his destiny. He would freely admit that he had sinned. He would admit that he was unworthy to be a son. And he would ask to be a hired servant.

(There were three classes of servants in Jewish society. Bondsmen were slaves who were a part of the estate, and indeed almost a part of the family. Underneath them in dignity were slaves of a lower class, subordinates to bondsmen. And finally, lowest of all, were hired servants -- casual day laborers from the village who had no continuing relationship with the family.)

He would claim nothing for himself but the status of hired servant. In this way, however, he could work for his living, and perhaps begin to make atonement for the mess he had made of his life.

There would be a problem, of course, in returning to the village. He had managed to offend the entire community by selling his inheritance while his father was living and he had lost his money to the Gentiles. His entry into the village would be humiliating, ruthless. But he would face the rejection. It would be part of the suffering he deserved, a way he could pay for his sins.

So he set off with his plan. He would live in the village as a servant; he would work to pay his own way; he would face the mockery of the village. But perhaps through it all he would be able to retain a certain amount of dignity -- at least within himself.

The prodigal's return is a perfect picture of the rabbi's teaching of repentance in Jesus' day. Repentance, in the Jewish mind, was a type of human work done to earn God's favor. God had to come part of the way, to be sure, but humans had to come the rest of the way. They had to do what they could. The work of repentance had to be sincere and accompanied by reparations for sin and a determination to avoid further sin. The prodigal planned a course of action which would fulfill the demands of repentance as taught by the rabbis.

Perhaps that's how you view the situation before you. You'd like to go home, to renew your relationship with the Father. So you develop a plan of action. You intend to do this and that, to become more regular in worship, to give more money to the church and charity, to clean up your life as best you can, and to face the music.

Maybe you are like the prodigal and already on the road home. Well be ready for a surprise.

The father knew what could happen if his son ever tried to return. He knew that a crowd could gather spontaneously as word of his return flashed through the gossip network. A sort of human barrier would be created at the edge of the village; he would be mocked, subjected to taunts, verbally and maybe even physically abused.

So when he heard the news, the father did what? He did what love amazing grace compelled him to do. He did not do what we would have expected him to do: he did not wait to see if the prodigal had learned his lesson; he did not wait to see if the prodigal was truly sorry for his wrongs; he did not wait for anything! He couldn't wait to do what he had to do, to do what he wanted to do!

He ran down the road to meet his son, to get to the edge of the village before his son. He ran. It was a horribly humiliating thing for a nobleman to run in the ancient east; it was a disgrace for a man of age to run down a road with robes flapping in the wind. Aristotle said, "Great men never run in public." But this father ran. His son was home!

He had to reach the edge of the village before his son. He knew what his son would face, so he ran to protect him. It was love compelling him, compassion for his son who had been lost but was now found.

The text literally says he fell on his son's neck and kissed him. Whenever a serious quarrel would break out in the village, part of the ceremony of reconciliation was for the leading men in the dispute to kiss each other. So the father kissed the son, taking the initiative in reconciliation, witnessing to the healing of the breach.

The returned prodigal started his speech, just as he had planned: "Father, I have sinned against heaven and before you; I am no longer worthy to be called your son." Then he stopped. He had planned to ask to become a hired servant, to be able to work for his living and pay his way as a resident in the village. But he said nothing of this. Why?

Most commentators think it's because the father interrupted him. I used to think that, but I've changed my mind. If the father had interrupted him the son could have finished his speech later in the story. And remember, Jesus could have told this story any way He wanted to tell it. The omission of the second half of the son's speech calls attention to itself; it must mean something important. Why didn't he follow through with his plan? What made the son change his mind?

I'll tell you what I think: he was shattered by the father's love. The unexpected welcome was overwhelming. The father had humiliated himself in the villagers' eyes; the father had taken the initiative and run to him; the father had announced reconciliation; the father had embraced him with compassion and forgiveness; the father had ... loved him with a love the son had never before recognized. It had always been there, but now it was evident. And the prodigal was overwhelmed. His plan was shattered. He knew he could not pay his way. The tragedy was not the lost money; the tragedy was a broken relationship which he could not heal but the father had healed out of love. Now he could not talk -- could not even think -- of being a hired servant. He was a son, and would always be a son.

The servants were told to get the "best robe" and put it on this poor, shivering wreck of a son. The best robe would be the father's own robe, the garment worn at all feasts and festive occasions. And the servants were told to find the ring -- the signet ring, the sign of family authority -- and to put it on his fingers, fingers that were still stinking of pig slop. And then the shoes. The servants were to get shoes out of his closet because sons wore shoes. Slaves did not wear shoes; only free men wore shoes. The robe, the ring, and shoes -- honor, authority, and freedom. Full restitution for the prodigal come home.

If all that wasn't enough, the father rounded out the instructions to his servants by telling them to get the fattest calf on the ranch and turn it into breaded veal. It was time to celebrate and have a party that would be talked about for years to come!

The choice of a calf is interesting. He could have slaughtered a goat; that would have provided plenty of food for a fine family celebration. But at least a hundred people would be required to eat a calf before it spoiled. The father intended to invite the whole village! The grandest banquet imaginable -- and everyone invited! The son had alienated the entire community, but now the entire community would come and make merry and the division would be healed. Reconciliation for all. Grace always leads to an inclusive party.

Do I need to say anything more? Perhaps you've been in a far country; perhaps you've developed a plan to get your life in order -- and even retain a bit of your dignity. But the Father awaits your return with a welcome that will overwhelm you with grace. See him running toward you now, feel the embrace and get ready for a welcoming party! Amen.

Sermon 6 - The Reason Jesus Came

It's a great privilege to be here. And to have all of you here. You have been faithful and stalwart friends. It's been really amazing and that is only from the Holy Spirit. I am grateful for your invitation.

I learned a verse of scripture from my Grandmother that you may know. John 3:16 "For God so loved the world that He gave his only begotten Son that whosoever believeth in him should not perish but have everlasting life."

In the beginning it says "For God"…You know, you can't put God in a test tube, you cannot prove scientifically that He exists, you can't see Him on a computer screen, but that doesn't mean that He is not real. He is the creator. Everything has been created by God. All the stars we see spread over the entire sky are part of the Milky Way Galaxy; but that galaxy is only a small fragment of the entire universe in which there are millions and billions of galaxies; and beyond what they thought was the last one.

Genesis, the first chapter tells us "In the beginning, God created the heavens and the earth…"and even here at the local zoo and local aquarium, that is one of the most beautiful in the world, you can see just a tiny fraction of the beautiful creatures that God has created. God is the creator of everything including you. God is a Spirit. God isn't a body like yours and mine. He's a Spirit, He can be everywhere at the same time. God is unchanging, the scripture says, "I am the Lord, I change not."

God is also holy. The scripture says, "God is Holy in all His works. Your eyes are too pure to look on evil. You cannot tolerate wrong, scripture says." God is also a judge. The bible says, "It is appointed unto man once to die, but after this the judgment." You are going to die. I am going to die. And after that, there will be a judgment. "Every idle word that men shall speak, they shall give an account thereof in the day of judgment", the scripture says.

When you break a law, you pay the price. You've broken God's law. We've broken the Ten Commandments and we're all sinners and we are all under the threat of judgment. There was a popular song years ago; "I won't stay in a world without love." You don't have to because God loves you. No matter what your sin or background, you can't do anything outside the love of God. Now God place man in a beautiful garden called Eden, he and his wife Eve were perfect; but one day they had a choice.

They had a choice to obey God or to disobey Him. They chose to disobey.

I do not understand how the devil became a serpent. I don't understand how terrible he must have been to lure Eve and Adam into sin. We know there is something wrong with human nature. Terrorism, war, greed, immorality, racial tensions. You know people used to look to technology to save them, now we are afraid that technology will destroy us.

Man has a terminal disease. Sin is the transgression of the law. How many of the Ten Commandments have you kept? Try to name them. We haven't kept many of them. The scripture says, all we like sheep have gone astray. We've turned every one to his own way. And the end of that kind of road is death; and judgment; and hell. The scripture says 'for the wages of sin is death, but the gift of God is eternal life through our Lord Jesus Christ'.

We are alienated from God. We are under the sentence of death. Are you ready to die? Whether you are a young person here today, or an old person like me, you'd better decide for Christ here and now; because you never know when your time is coming to leave this world. You know God loves us...so much...and...

… one day I was walking with one of my sons. Down the mountain path and we stepped on an ant hill. A lot of ants were suffering and their little house had been destroyed. And we got down and looked and I thought to myself, I wish we could go down and help them rebuild; or help the ants get to a hospital. But we couldn't, we were too big and they were too little. God looked down on this planet and saw us as little ants, He saw that we were destroying ourselves…and God decided to become a man…and that's who Jesus Christ was…He was God in the flesh. He came to tell us that He loved us.

He taught us many wonderful things, He healed many sick people…He taught us the way to heaven. He taught us that we could have peace and joy and happiness in this life.

The scripture says, when He died on the cross, and shed His blood for us; He has made Him to be sin for us. Think of it; Jesus Christ became sin. When He looked in that cup at Gethsemane, what did He see? He said, 'if it be possible, let this cup pass from me'. And that cup was the sins of the whole world including yours and mine, for He has made Him to be sin for us.

Then in Isaiah it says, 'the Lord laid on Him the iniquity of us all'.

In 1st Peter 2 it says, 'Through His own self, bear our own sins in His own body on the cross'. Then in Peter it says, 'Christ also once suffered for sin, the just for the unjust'. But the cross was not the end. They buried Him. Three days later He rose from the dead.

And Jesus said, "I am the resurrection and the life, he that believeth on me though he were dead, yet shall he live. And whosoever liveth and believeth in me shall never die". And the scripture says, 'if we confess with our mouth the Lord Jesus and shall believe in thine heart that God raised Him from the dead, thou shall be saved'.

That's not the end of the story. The end of the story is when you come to Christ. And then the coming again of Jesus.

My mother used to tell me that every morning when she woke up, she thought this may be the day when He was coming back. I thought that many times myself; this may be the day.

Hereafter shall ye see the Son of man sitting on the right hand of power and coming in the clouds in heaven. Now what do you have to do? God has done all that for us, what do we have to do?

First, you must repent of your sins. The first sermon Jesus ever preached was repentance. Scripture says He began to preach and to say, 'Repent for the kingdom of heaven is at hand. Repentance means we are sorry enough to quit. Repent there and be converted that your sins may be blotted out.

God commands all people everywhere to repent the scripture says. It means to turn around. To change your mind. To head in a new direction in your life, now only must you repent but you must believe. Without faith, it is impossible to please Him. For he that cometh to God must belive that He is...

In Ephesians it says, 'for by grace you are saved through faith; the word faith means commitment; you are committed to Christ. It is not a blind irrational leap into the dark because Jesus Christ took your place and paid the penalty for you. You can start over again; start life all over right here today. I'm going to ask you to do something that we have seen thousands of people do in different parts of the world. I'm going to ask you to say I do want my life to change. I want to be certain that if I died I'd go to heaven. I'm going to ask you to come and make this decision. Make certain that you know Christ as your Lord and Saviour. You may want to rededicate your life, you come.

Sermon 7 - Where Is Your Treasure?

There is an old film entitled 'The End' which starred Burt Reynolds. In this film, the lead character played by Reynolds decides to commit suicide by swimming out as far as he can until he is exhausted and then just let himself sink under the waves. But after going under he is looking up at the surface from beneath the waves and decides not to go through with it. As he breaks up above the surface of the water he screams: "I want to live! I want to live!"

He then begins to try to swim to shore, but he realizes it is a very long way off. As he begins to swim he starts to talk to God. He promises to obey all of the Ten Commandments, and then quickly realizes he doesn't know what all of them are so he promises to learn them. Then, in his panic, he says, "Lord, if you get me out of this, I will give you 80% of everything I have!"

But the time passes and he is still going strong swimming towards shore, and besides he can just begin to see the shoreline. But as he continues to swim he feels his strength growing a bit better and says, "Lord, if you help me to get to shore alive I will give you 10% of everything I earn." And, finally, as he struggles to the place where he sees that he is just going to be able to make it to land he says, "Well, Lord, let's just forget about what I said before. I think I can make it from here on my own."

The attitude of the character played by Reynolds is reflective of the attitude of many people today. Giving to God or living for God are sometimes thought of as "paying our dues," or fulfilling an obligation. What should our attitude toward giving be? What is the proper way to give and think about giving?

The first point we need to understand is: Giving is an act of worship. It is an expression of gratitude to a faithful God for all his goodness to me. Giving is not just a response to a need in the church, it is a response of gratitude. It is giving as though we were placing it in God's hands. Worship is a word that comes from the word "worthy." We give to God because he is Lord of the universe and he is worthy of our praise. We worship him with our lips, with our gifts and with our lives. The question often arises: How much should I give? To answer that question we have to look to the Scripture.

First of all let's examine the Old Testament. Leviticus 27:30 says, "A tithe of everything from the land, whether grain from the soil or fruit from the trees, belongs to the LORD; it is holy to the LORD." The Old Testament standard of giving was the tithe, and this principle is found many places throughout the Old Testament. It was among the earliest laws of the Israelites. The idea was that 10% of what they owned belonged to God, therefore it was holy. It was to be set aside for him and not used for common purposes. It was sacred. God was claiming ownership of 10% of everything the Israelites owned. They had worked for their food and money, but it was God who blessed them with crops and herds, and the ability to work. Out of gratefulness to him they were to return a tenth of everything to him. And when they acknowledged God's ownership of 10% of their belongings God made a promise. Malachi 3:10 says, "'Bring the whole tithe into the storehouse, that there may be food in my house. Test me in this,' says the LORD Almighty, 'and see if I will not throw open the floodgates of heaven and pour out so much blessing that you will not have room enough for it.'"

You may say, "Yes, that is all very well and good, but that is the Old Testament. What about the New Testament? Tithing is not even mentioned in the New Testament." You are correct. The New Testament standard for giving is not the tithe. The New Testament has a totally different pattern for stewardship than the Old Testament. To understand the New Testament concept of giving we have to look at the story of the Rich Young Ruler. This young man came to Jesus in search of heaven, and asked Jesus what he had to do to inherit eternal life. Jesus' response was to explain that he must first follow the basic laws of God — the ten commandments. The young man replied that he had kept all of the commandments from his youth. And then Jesus completely astounded him by saying, "Go, sell your possessions and give to the poor, and you will have treasure in heaven. Then come, follow me" (Matthew 19:21). The Bible sadly reports, "When the young man heard this, he went away sad, because he had great wealth."

What was Jesus saying to this young man? He was giving the New Testament principle of stewardship, and that principle is this: Whereas the Old Testament taught us that 10% of everything we own belongs to God, the New Testament, and in particular Jesus, is teaching us that ALL we have belongs to God. The Old Testament was a partial picture of a greater truth. The Old Testament showed us that God had certain claims on our lives, but the New Testament shows us the full extent of those claims. God does not just own a part of me; he owns all of me. To acknowledge this and live this way is an act of worship.

Let's look at another New Testament example of this principle.

The Bible tells the story of the widow's mite in this way, "Jesus sat down opposite the place where the offerings were put and watched the crowd putting their money into the temple treasury. Many rich people threw in large amounts. But a poor widow came and put in two very small copper coins, worth only a fraction of a penny. Calling his disciples to him, Jesus said, 'I tell you the truth, this poor widow has put more into the treasury than all the others. They all gave out of their wealth; but she, out of her poverty, put in everything — all she had to live on'" (Mark 12:41-44). When we read this story we usually emphasize the smallness of her gift — that it was only a fraction of a penny. But the point is not how small her gift was, but how BIG it was. The gift of the wealthy was small by comparison, because they did not give all they had, as she did. That is the New Testament principle of giving. When we come into contact with God we dare not be stingy for we serve a great and awesome God. As an act of worship we acknowledge that he owns all that we have.

Jesus said, "Freely you have received, freely give" (Matthew 10:8). The point is not whether you will literally give away all you have, but whether or not you recognize God's complete and unconditional ownership of all you possess. We are talking about an entirely new attitude toward life. This is true worship.

The second point is this: Giving tells me where my heart is. Jesus always demanded everything from his followers, and there were many who were not willing to pay the price. Do you remember those who said they were willing to follow Jesus wherever he would go? He turned them back knowing that they were not willing to pay the cost. He said things like, "Foxes have holes and birds of the air have nests, but the Son of Man has no place to lay his head." When they heard this they no longer followed him. But what about the true disciples, the twelve? Peter said to Jesus, "We have left all we had to follow you!" And Jesus said to him, "I tell you the truth, no one who has left home or wife or brothers or parents or children for the sake of the kingdom of God will fail to receive many times as much in this age and, in the age to come, eternal life" (Luke 18:28-30).

Unreserved commitment results in unrestrained blessing. When you hold nothing back from God he holds nothing back from you. If we do not withhold from God our material blessings, he will not withhold from us his spiritual blessings. The danger for us who live in a materialistic society is that we will value material things more than spiritual things.

I was watching the News Hour with Jim Lehrer the other evening, and he was discussing how the candidates ran their campaigns with Mark Shields and Paul Gigot and two other analysts on the Roundtable segment. Sheilds and Gigot are antagonists, with Sheilds being the liberal and Gigot the conservative. During the discussion Mark Shields made a profound and eloquent observation which seemed to be lost with the other pundits. He said, "It was a campaign devoid of any poetry. It was a campaign where sacrifice was never whispered. There was no mention of duty — of what any of us owes to each other, to our country. ...It was a campaign about interests. It was basically about, 'This is your interest. You want it, you got it.' In that sense both of them missed a marvelous opportunity, in a time of great prosperity, to touch what is good in the American people and summon us to a higher level." In other words, it was all about us: our social security, our taxes, our prosperity, our surplus. There was no call to do something wonderful like revitalize the Peace Corps and flood the world with an army of compassion.

But sacrifice is not a message that seems to fit in a time of prosperity. David Broder observed during the same discussion, "These are not times which call for great emotion or even great idealism." How sad! Why shouldn't peace and prosperity be the times of highest idealism?

Because prosperity turns our focus on ourselves and dulls our higher senses. The challenge should be that since we have so much, in the words of John Kennedy, we should not be asking what our country can do for us, but what we can do for our country. We should be asking what we can do for those who live in abject poverty in other places and how we can make the world a better place with the tremendous resources at our disposal.

I have been thinking a lot lately about why the people of the United States have so little time for spiritual things. Generally speaking, there is not much evidence of a widespread passion for God and the things of his kingdom. People in Korea and other places in the world spend hours in prayer on a daily basis. The churches of China, Africa and South America are growing exponentially because of the enormous spiritual hunger of the people. Their worship is enthusiastic and even electric. Why is that not more the case here in the United States where we have experienced so much of God's blessing?

We who have been so blessed by God should be more full of worship than anyone else. The answer to this question, I believe, lies in the fact that the sin of materialism has blunted our spiritual desires. When we do feel a spiritual longing, we have so much with which we can artificially soothe the deep needs of our lives. We buy something new, or indulge in some pleasure or interest. We keep ourselves so busy that we could not possibly get in touch with the deep spiritual longings of our lives. Isn't it interesting that the more we have the more we want, and the less grateful we are? The more we have the more likely we are to keep it to ourselves.

We all believe that we can handle the temptations that accompany material wealth, but the truth is that for every ten people who can handle poverty only one can handle prosperity. Jesus said, "No one can serve two masters. Either he will hate the one and love the other, or he will be devoted to the one and despise the other. You cannot serve both God and Money" (Matthew 6:24).

Jesus told the story of the rich fool who stored up his material goods and said to himself: "You have plenty of good things laid up for many years. Take life easy; eat, drink and be merry." But then God said to him, "You fool! This very night your life will be demanded from you. Then who will get what you have prepared for yourself?" God forbid that those words be spoken to us, for Jesus closed the story with these words: "This is how it will be with anyone who stores up things for himself but is not rich toward God" (Luke 12:19-21). What is your attitude toward money and possessions? The Bible says, "Every good and perfect gift is from above, coming down from the Father of the heavenly lights, who does not change like shifting shadows" (James 1:17). Giving pries our fingers from our money and possessions and begins to free us from the slavery of greed and materialism.

The third point we need to understand is: Giving is an indicator of how much I trust God. If I think I have to do it all myself, and that God is not a rewarder of those who trust him, then I am not living as God wants me to live. The Bible says, "And without faith it is impossible to please God, because anyone who comes to him must believe that he exists and that he rewards those who earnestly seek him" (Hebrews 11:6). As Christians we are assured that God is aware of our needs and will take care of us. Jesus said, "If that is how God clothes the grass of the field, which is here today and tomorrow is thrown into the fire, will he not much more clothe you, O you of little faith? So do not worry, saying, 'What shall we eat?' or 'What shall we drink?' or 'What shall we wear?' For the pagans run after all these things, and your heavenly Father knows that you need them. But seek first his kingdom and his righteousness, and all these things will be given to you as well" (Matthew 6:30). If I don't believe that down deep in my heart I will never be able to give at any meaningful level. The Bible says, "Whoever sows sparingly will also reap sparingly, and whoever sows generously will also reap generously" (2 Corinthians 9:6). We can be generous in our giving because we have a God who cares for us and provides for us. The more we seek the things of the Spirit, the less material things mean to us. We still use them and enjoy them, but we recognize Who has given them to us. We understand that we do not own them. We are merely stewards of these things, and we keep a loose grip on them.

Almost all the Bible has to say about money is negative, unless it is talking about giving it away. The Bible is positive when it says, "It is more blessed to give than to receive" (Acts 20:35). And it is also positive when it says, "Each man should give what he has decided in his heart to give, not reluctantly or under compulsion, for God loves a cheerful giver" (2 Corinthians 9:7). But the Bible constantly warns about the spiritual danger that is caused by having money. It says, "For the love of money is a root of all kinds of evil. Some people, eager for money, have wandered from the faith and pierced themselves with many griefs" (1 Timothy 6:10). Hebrews 13:5 says, "Keep your lives free from the love of money and be content with what you have, because God has said, 'Never will I leave you; never will I forsake you.'" No one ever ruined their character by being too generous, but many people have ruined their character because of the love of money.

John Wesley, the founder of the Methodist Church, said, "Get all you can, save all you can, give all you can." We say "Get all you can, can all you get, and sit on the lid." We do not trust God to provide our needs. Do you remember the people of Israel in the Sinai desert? They needed food and God gave them manna. Each day they were to go out and collect as much manna as they needed for one day — no more, no less. Those who collected little found it to be enough, but there were those who collected more than they needed and tried to store it in jars. But when they went to the jars the next day to eat the manna they found it to be rotten and full of maggots. What was the lesson the Israelites were to learn through all of this? It was that the Lord was their supply. They were to put their trust in God for their provision on a daily basis, and not allow their provisions to be their security and their god. They were to look to him for their security and not their stored supplies. There are many people today who are trusting their bank accounts rather than God. They have placed their security and trust in something other than the Lord. We even call them "securities" and "trusts."

Jesus said, "Do not store up for yourselves treasures on earth, where moth and rust destroy, and where thieves break in and steal. But store up for yourselves treasures in heaven, where moth and rust do not destroy, and where thieves do not break in and steal. For where your treasure is, there your heart will be also" (Matthew 6:17).

Where is your treasure? Is it invested in yourself, in possessions or pleasures? Is it hidden away in banks and securities, or is it invested in the kingdom of God where it will be used for his work? When we give to God, it reminds us from where the things we have come. Where you spend your money is an accurate gauge of what you value in life and where the things of real importance are to you. Have you invested in the material or spiritual?

How we give demonstrates whether we are trusting God, or whether our security lies elsewhere. The things on which you spend your money and where your treasure is invested is very important, because Jesus said, "where your treasure is, there your heart will be also."

Sermon 8 - Notes on Giving

A wealthy older gentleman had just recently married a lovely young lady, and was beginning to wonder whether she might have married him for his money. So he asked her, "Tell me the truth: if I lost all my money, would you still love me?" She said reassuringly, "Oh honey, don't be silly. Of course I would still love you. And I'd miss you terribly."

Money can change your attitude and who you are as a person.

There is a story about a guy who came to church with his family. As they were driving home afterwards he was complaining about everything. He said, "The music was too loud. The sermon was too long. The announcements were unclear. The building was hot. The people were unfriendly." He went on & on, complaining about virtually everything. Finally, his very observant son said, "Dad, you've got to admit it wasn't a bad show for just a dollar."

Average annual income in India is $1000 a year.

Average annual income in Afghanistan. $800 a year.

Wealthiest nation on earth. Americans are taken care of. 1/2% of our population controls 40% of our nation's wealth.

Why does God bless Christians? Part of the promise was that all nations would look to you and see that you are taken care of very nicely. It is because they share the wealth.

So the question this morning is: Does your giving reflect greatness?

- A Barna research study back in April 2000 found that only 8% of Christians give 10% of their income or more.

According to statistics, in American Churches the breakdown of giving looks like this:

20% of members Give 80% of all funds

30% of members Give the other 20%

50% of members Give nothing – ever!

I don't know if that's true here I doubt it, and I hope it isn't.

John Wesley, the founder of the Methodist Church, said, "Get all you can, save all you can, give all you can." We say "Get all you can, can all you get, and sit on the lid."

Martin Luther said, I have tried to keep things in my hands and lost them all, but what I have given into God's hands I still possess.

The roof of the church hall of a little Swiss church, at the turn of the 20th century, was falling down. So the members of the church held regular prayer meetings in the hall after the service to pray for funds to repair the roof.

There was an old man, known to be very tight with his money, who used to attend and sit near the back of the hall. He could sneak out just before the collection plate came round at the end of the prayer meeting.

One Sunday, he was held up on his way to the prayer meeting in the Hall by the vicar and could only find a seat at the front of the church.

During the prayer meeting, a piece of the roof fell and hit him on the head. Feeling spoke to by the Lord, he stood up and said "Lord, I'll give $1000"

A voice at the back of the church was heard to say "Hit him again, Lord"!

God is a gentleman and He isn't going to beat you or cause misfortune if you don't give, but He patiently reminds us that He has asked us to give to Him

How should I give?

Luke 21:1-4 1 As he looked up, Jesus saw the rich putting their gifts into the temple treasury. 2 He also saw a poor widow put in two very small copper coins. 3 "I tell you the truth," he said, "this poor widow has put in more than all the others. 4 all these people gave their gifts out of their wealth; but she out of her poverty put in all she had to live on."

People who give sacrificially know where their money came from.

Jimmy Stewart in the movie Shanendoah plays a farmer who has a bunch of sons. The Boys are of fighting age and the father will not let them go off to fight. The family gets the reputation of sitting out the war. There is a scene where they are all around the dinner table and they bow their heads for prayer. Jimmy Stewart says "Lord we planted this seed, we watered the plants, we picked the food and we cooked it, we did it all ourselves, we worked dog bone hard for this but we thank you just the same amen"

People who give sacrificially know that they worked hard for what they take home, but they also know that God blessed them and provided for them.

When you give sacrificially you are saying "Lord I want you to be God of my whole life, and my giving needs to reflect that."

People who give sacrificially trust in God to provide

They are not only socially secure in Jesus they are spiritually secure in Jesus as well.

Colossians 4:2 Devote yourselves to prayer, being watchful and thankful.

Pray that your gift will be used in a great way.

Thank God for what He has used your gifts for.

Matthew 6:1-4 1 "Be careful not to do your 'acts of righteousness' before men, to be seen by them. If you do, you will have no reward from your Father in heaven. 2 "So when you give to the needy, do not announce it with trumpets, as the hypocrites do in the synagogues and on the streets, to be honored by men. I tell you the truth, they have received their reward in full. 3 But when you give to the needy, do not let your left hand know what your right hand is doing, 4 so that your giving may be in secret. Then your Father, who sees what is done in secret, will reward you.

You don't need to tell everyone what the amount of your gift is. It a private matter.

There is an old story about a king that was coming to visit a certain land. The people in the land were so excited that a king would grace their little village with his presence. They wanted to find a way to honor him, and decided to do so by giving him the best of their wine. Every person was to bring one cup of their best wine from home and they would all put it in one big pot, and when the king came he would taste the best wine from all the people. One person thought if everyone else is bringing their best then I could bring water, it won't make a bit of difference with hundreds of others bringing their best. When the king arrived and tasted the wine, he discovered that it was all water. The king was not honored.

I know that when I have prepared to give, Satan has said to me "you don't have to give all that, nobody will notice if you don't give." But if we give only water that the king will not be honored

In Malachi 3 God is angry. One of the things that has happened is that His people have not honored him with their money.

Malachi 3:10 Bring the whole tithe into the storehouse, that there may be food in my house. Test me in this," says the LORD Almighty, "and see if I will not throw open the floodgates of heaven and pour out so much blessing that you will not have room enough for it.

Get real about what you give.

Ann Landers had an interesting letter in her column. It was from a girl who was writing about her uncle & aunt. She said, "My uncle was the tightest man I've ever known. All his life, every time he got paid he took $20 out of his paycheck & put it under his mattress.

Then he got sick & was about to die. As he was dying, he said to his wife, "I want you to promise me one thing." "Promise what?" she asked. "I want you to promise me that when I'm dead you'll take my money from under the mattress & put it in my casket so that I can take it all with me."

"He died, & his wife kept her promise. She went in & got all that money the day he died & went to the bank & deposited it, & wrote out a check & put it in his casket."

God wants us to be realistic about money.

He wants us to be realistic about what we give. His desire is that we make a realistic responsible commitment to him.

Juan Carlos was a famous pirate he was notorious for his thievery and it was rumored that he had a very large amount of plunder buried. One day he was in Mexico and a man came up to him and pushed him to the ground and said "Juan Carlos tell me where all your money is buried or I will shoot you right here" Juan Carlos didn't speak a word of English and he knew that he knew he was going to need an interpreter so he found a boy. The boy relayed the message to Juan Carlos and fearing for his life Juan Carlos said "tell him that I don't want to die and the money is located 30 paces north of the city water tower under a large rock". So the boy turned to the man and said, "Juan Carlos says he is an honorable man and he will never tell you where the money is he says to kill him now."

God's desire is that you are honest about your finances as well.

Did you know Jesus talked about money more than he talked about heaven? In Matthew, Mark, and Luke: 1 out of every 6 verses deals with money. Of the 29 parables Christ told, 16 deal with a person and his money.

Why did Jesus talk about Money so much? Because He wants us to be realistic about money.

We understand things in terms of dollars. But God also promises to honor our gifts in this verse.

On the last day of school, children were bringing gifts to their teacher. The florist's son brought the teacher a bouquet. The candy store owner's son brought the teacher a pretty box of candy. Then the liquor store owner's son brought a big, heavy box. The teacher lifted it up and noticed that it was leaking a little bit. She touched a drop of the liquid with her finger and tasted it. "Is it wine?" She guessed. "No," said the boy. She tasted another drop and asked, "Champagne?" "No," said the little boy. "It's a puppy!"

Can you anticipate what God wants to give you, what kind of gift he has for you?

If you don't give a tenth you should start. Be realistic about what God is asking of you.

J.L. Kraft, head of the Kraft Cheese Corporation, who had given approximately 25% of his enormous income to Christian causes for many years, said, "The only investment I ever made which has paid consistently increasing dividends is the money I have given to the Lord."

J.D. Rockefeller said, "I never would have been able to tithe the first million dollars I ever made if I had not tithed my first salary, which was $1.50 per week."

Luke 6:38 says give, and it will be given to you. A good measure, pressed down, shaken together and running over, will be poured into your lap. For with the measure you use, it will be measured to you."

Tony Campolo tells a story of a homeless man who offered to share his coffee with Tony. Tony said the coffee must have been swimming with bacteria but he took a drink. Then he said "that's very generous of you to share your coffee with me." And the man said "I believe that when God gives you something extra special you should share it".

Three boys in the school yard were bragging about who had the better father. The first boy says, "My Dad scribbles a few words on a piece of paper, he calls it a song, and they give him $500." The second boy says, "That's nothing. My Dad scribbles a few words on a piece of paper, he calls it a brief, and they give him $1000." The third boy says, "My Dad is even better than that. He scribbles a few words on a piece of paper, calls it a sermon, and it takes six men just to collect all the money!"

Some of your money goes to pay the minister, but some of it goes to missions in fact an unprecedented amount of your giving goes to missions. Some of it goes for building upkeep, and some goes to paying for curriculum. Every dollar that you give goes to an area of ministry. Ministry Costs Money, and the more generous you are the more ministry we can do.

Rick Stacy tells the people at Meridian Christian Church in Lansing that you shouldn't give because you think you have to or God needs your money. Because that will always be true, The church that does ministry will always have expenses, And those expenses are going to keep growing. He says you should give because you love God and you want to invest in Him and the kingdom He has created. The more you give the more ministries that can be done.

If the Church today is going to be effective, it must take measurable progressive steps forward. These steps cannot be taken by one person alone, but rather they must be taken together as a group.

2 Corinthians 9:5 So I thought it necessary to urge the brothers to visit you in advance and finish the arrangements for the generous gift you had promised. Then it will be ready as a generous gift, not as one grudgingly given.

I believe that God asks us to give a little more so he can bless us a little more.

So what I am asking you to do is this

If you don't tithe, consider starting. If you do tithe consider an increase.
God will Honor your gift.

Matthew 6:19-24 19 "Do not store up for yourselves treasures on earth, where moth and rust destroy, and where thieves break in and steal. But store up for yourselves treasures in heaven, where moth and rust do not destroy, and where thieves do not break in and steal. For where your treasure is, there your heart will be also. "The eye is the lamp of the body. If your eyes are good, your whole body will be full of light. But if your eyes are bad, your whole body will be full of darkness. If then the light within you is darkness, how great is that darkness! "No one can serve two masters. Either he will hate the one and love the other, or he will be devoted to the one and despise the other. You cannot serve both God and Money.

In other words You should give to a heavenly cause,
Well I have good news
The Church is God's heavenly cause here and now. So when you give here you are putting a down payment on the future of this church.

A sailor was shipwrecked on a South Sea Island. He was seized by the natives, carried shoulder-high to throne, and proclaimed king. He learned that according to their custom the king ruled for a year.

The idea appealed to the sailor until he wondered what had happened to all the previous kings. Then he learned that when a king's reign ended, he was banished to a lonely island to starve to death.

So, knowing he was king for the year, this sailor began issuing orders. Carpenters were to make boats. Farmers were to go ahead to this island and plant crops.

Builders were to erect a home. When his reign finished, he was exiled, not to a barren isle, but to a paradise of plenty.

Let me ask you; Do you view your contribution as paying for the past or financing the future?

You say what's the difference, a church that's paying for the past is struggling to meet the needs of yesterday. Finally paying for the ministry they did years ago.

A person who is paying for the past is giving so that the Glory days of old will return.

There is nothing wrong with memories, and recalling the good times But we can't stay locked in that mindset. I firmly believe that God is calling us to finance the future.

A church that finances the future is a church that invests in the young people of today.

A church that finances the future is a church that looks at where God is currently and then joins him there; a church that finances the future is a church that anticipates where God is going and prepares to go there as well.

The Jewish temple treasury in Jesus day had 13 places to give offering they were called trumpets because they looked like trumpets.

Underneath them they had a label that said what that certain fund was used for. Much like our designated funds are today. The people were used to giving with a purpose and I encourage you to give with purpose as well. So if you desire your gift to go to a specific area of ministry there in nothing wrong with that.

2 Corinthians 9:7 Each man should give what he has decided in his heart to give, not reluctantly or under compulsion, for God loves a cheerful giver.

An attitude of giving translates into an attitude of ministry.

God you are going to do great things with this Church, and I am confident that you will do great things with my gift.

A man on vacation was strolling along outside his hotel in Acapulco, enjoying the sunny Mexican weather. He heard the screams of a woman kneeling in front of a child. The man knew enough Spanish to determine that the boy had swallowed a coin. Seizing the child by the heels, the man held him up, gave him a few shakes, and an American quarter dropped to the sidewalk. "Oh, thank you sir!" cried the woman. "You seemed to know just how to get it out of him. Are you a doctor?" "No, ma'am, " replied the man. "I'm with the United States Internal Revenue Service."

God is a Gentleman and he isn't going to make the building fall on you, He is not going to pick you up and shake you out, there will be no spiritual audit on your checkbook.

The Bible says that Giving is part of your act of worship. So if it's worth it to read your bible daily; if it's worth it to have the security of Him hearing your prayer; if it's worth it to come this place and worship; if it's worth it to have friends that are grounded in His word .Shouldn't it be worth it to honor Him financially as well?

The famous psychiatrist, Karl Menninger has stated that one sign of mental health is the ability to release money -- give it away. Think -- How many generous people do you know who exhibit mental instability? It is often the stingy, controlling person who is neurotic. God created us to be healthy. One way to contribute to your mental health is to practice generosity.

A boy and his mother were in a drug store and there was candy on the counter and the owner spotted the boy looking at the candy, when the mother went up to pay the owner said to the boy "you want some of this candy". The boy nodded, and the manager said well go "ahead and take some". Well the boy just stood there, and again the owner said "go ahead and get a handful of candy". The boy still stood there then the owner reached in the jar and pulled out some candy and gave it to the boy and the boy filled his pockets. When they got outside the mother said why didn't you get a handful of candy the man told you it was O.K.. And the boy said, "because his hands were bigger than mine".

Let me ask you: Whose hands do you want to rely on?

*** Additional Notes on Giving ***

Henry Ford, the American industrialist, was once asked to donate money for the construction of a new medical facility. The billionaire agreed and pledged to donate $5,000. The next day in the newspaper, the headlines read, "Henry Ford contributes $50,000 to the local hospital."

Ford was irritated at the obvious mistake and was on the phone immediately to complain to the fund-raiser that he had been misunderstood. The fund-raiser replied that they would print a retraction in the paper the following day to read, "Henry Ford reduces his donation by $45,000." Realizing the poor publicity that would result, the industrialist agreed to the $50,000 contribution in return for the following: That above the entrance to the hospital was to be carved the biblical inscription: "I came among you and you took me in."

Sometimes in life we feel like we've been taken in or we've been took! Ever make a bad purchase? Ever buy a lemon? Ever give to a cause that you knew was going nowhere? Ever give to a person whom you knew would blow it?

To give or not to give? That is usually the question. Actually, that is not the question. That may be the question for many people in our world, but it should not be for the Christian. As Christians, giving should be a natural part of our lives. We should want to give because of God's example of giving to us.

John 3:16 "For God so loved the world that He gave..."

God has given everything for our enjoyment in this life and He has given us what it takes to make it to eternity. The greatest of all gifts is the sacrifice of His son Jesus on the cross. Giving doesn't get any better than that.

No matter how much we give back to God through the church or missions or by any others means, we will never outdistance His giving. But this doesn't mean that we should stop giving or cut back in our giving.

The well known Preacher W.A. Criswell told of an ambitious young man who told his pastor he'd promised God a tithe of his income. They prayed for God to bless his career. At that time he was making $40.00 per week and tithing $4.00. In a few years his income increased and he was tithing $500.00 per week.

He called on the pastor to see if he could be released from his tithing promise, it was too costly now. The pastor replied, "I don't see how you can be released from your promise, but we can ask God to reduce your income to $40.00 a week, then you'd have no problem tithing $4.00."

That doesn't figure, does it? You would think that as a person is blessed by God financially they would want to give even more back to God. This story just reminds us of how self-centered we really are.

Ever heard of Jon M. Huntsman? He is a billionaire who gave $100 million dollars to help find a cure for cancer. Huntsman has gone through two bouts of cancer himself. He had prostate cancer in 1992 and then cancer of the mouth in 1993.

It's said that Huntsman could be a poster boy for old-fashioned values. He grew up in what he describes as a "humble and modest" home in Blackfoot, Idaho, the second of three sons of a schoolteacher and his wife.

How do you think he made his billion dollars? One thing was the "Big Mac" plastic burger box for McDonald's. I think prior to that it was the egg carton and then came plastic bowls and plates for hospital use. His companies are in 23 different countries. Huntsman said, "I never dreamed that I would be in this position financially someday, nor did our family ever expect it, nor do I think, frankly, that we deserve it."

"But it's unfolded in such an incredible way, I feel maybe the good Lord intended me to utilize it for the betterment of human-kind. There's no better explanation for someone to have picked potatoes as a kid and suddenly have a $4 to $5 billion dollar company in one lifetime."

Huntsman has done a good thing. His giving has apparently been motivated by a gracious God. And so must our giving be.

It's been said that when we give we are most like God. This may very well be. Giving is one of the hardest things for most people to do, because we are taking away from ourselves. And self is very strong in all of us. Self will so often dominate and control our actions.

So when it comes to giving in any form, let's think in terms of becoming more like God and Christ who have given their all for us and to us.

Now for some more motivation. Does it do any good to give to others or for the cause of Christ?

In Philippians, Paul tells us what our giving will do for others and us. Phil 4 Verse 14 "Yet it was good of you to share in my troubles.

It's like what the preacher told the young couple about to get married, "One of you should know how to write a check. Because, even if you have tons of love, there is still going to be a lot of bills." We all know that two people cannot live cheaper than one!

Most everyone experiences some kind of trouble in life, but not everyone experiences financial troubles. There are a few people who are blessed financially.

I had one man in a church tell me that he'd always had a very good job that paid well. They never wanted for anything. If they wanted something, they just went out and bought it. That's nice, but doesn't happen with most of us. And it didn't happen with Paul either. He knew what it was to be in need and what it was to abound at times.

Sophie Tucker a vaudeville entertainer is quoted as saying:

From birth to eighteen, a girl needs good parents.

From eighteen to thirty-five, she needs good looks.

From thirty-five to fifty-five, she needs a good personality.

From fifty-five on, she needs cash.

Most people need cash occasionally. Paul needed cash or some kind of financial support in his missionary and evangelism ministry.

Whenever we give to someone in need we bless them. Paul said it was good that they shared in his financial troubles. It's always a blessing to people when they have a need and we can help with that need. It helps to lift the burden.

Romans 12:13 "Share with God's people who are in need."

Galatians 6:9-10 "Let us not become weary in doing good, for at the proper time we will reap a harvest if we do not give up. Therefore, as we have opportunity, let us do good to all people, especially to those who belong to the family of believers."

Prov. 3:27 "Do not withhold good from those who deserve it, when it is in your power to act." God has given us the power to act, to do good, to share, etc.

When do you feel best about yourself in life? When you do good? When you do something for someone else? When you help another person in need? When you give to someone in need? Yes, it's true and it's because God made us to care for one another. God wants us to bless one another and that's what our giving will do.

Philippians 4 Verse 17 "Not that I am looking for a gift, but I am looking for what may be credited to your account."

How's your account? Not that good? Mine isn't either! How I wish! How we all wish!

But more important than our bank account is our heavenly account. How's that account? Didn't you know that you had one? According to this text and others, you do.

Matt. 6:19-20 Jesus said, "Do not store up for yourselves treasures on earth, where moth and rust destroy, and where thieves break in and steal. But store up for yourselves treasures in heaven, where moth and rust do not destroy, and where thieves do not break in and steal."

Apparently, we all have some kind of heavenly account, in which hopefully we are making deposits.

Bob Russell of the large Southeast Christian Church, Louisville, KY, said on the radio some years ago that Christians in America give 4 billion dollars a year to their churches. Sounds good doesn't it? It is good. Sounds very good until you hear that those same Christian people spend something like 34 billion dollars a year on diet and exercise products.

I am reminded of the story about the wealthy, but very selfish lady who died and went to heaven. She was told that she would be taken to the house, which had been prepared for her. She passed by many beautiful mansions and saw in them, people whom in this life had been very poor and somewhat rejected by others. Finally, on the very outskirts of heaven she was shown a very small, rundown house and was told it was hers. She complained and protested, but she was told, "We're sorry, but this is all we could do for you with the materials you sent up."

I Tim. 6:18-19 "Command them to do good, to be rich in good deeds, and to be generous and willing to share. In this way they will lay up treasure for themselves as a firm foundation for the coming age, so that they may take hold of the life that is truly life."

What will our giving do? Apparently, we have some kind of account in heaven. The important thing is to make deposits and we do this by giving, not by saving or hoarding.

Philippians 4 Verse 18 "They (the Philippians' gift to Paul) are a fragrant offering, an acceptable sacrifice, pleasing to God."

Heb. 13:16 "And do not forget to do good and to share with others, for which such sacrifices God is pleased."

One day when I was in elementary school I went home with a friend after school. I was told to come home as soon as school was out. Why did I go home with George Huffman instead of going to my own home? I don't know. I liked George and I wanted to play more than I wanted to go home.

However, when George took me home on his new bike after we had finished playing, I saw my dad standing in the front yard, waiting for me. He was not happy. I had not pleased my father and he quickly demonstrated his displeasure with his belt.

I remember that as a teenager in high school I would lift my homemade weights outside the house. Dad thought it was somewhat foolish. I think he thought I would gain more muscle and do more good by working. I did not please my father.

When I was about 18 years old, I wrecked my car while driving to work at 10 p.m. I worked the night shift at Safeway, 10 p.m. to 7 a.m. I went between a telephone pole and the guy wire, and then mowed down a farmer's wooden fence. My 1955 Chevy was totaled. I was fortunate and only had a few bruises and a huge bruised pride. I crawled out of the car and asked the farmer if I could use his phone to call my dad. Dad was not happy but he came to get me and take me to work. The next morning he picked me up from work. Again, you guessed it, I did not please my father.

Now, you may be thinking, "I wonder if he ever pleased his father?" Hopefully, I did, but I don't recall. It's sad to think that we don't know if we ever pleased our parents and that's because they never told us we did.

Commending a child is just as important as criticizing a child and perhaps more important. Children need commendation in life and more than we realize.

Matt. 4:17 "And a voice from heaven said, 'This is my Son, whom I love; with him I have well pleased.'"

After Jesus was baptized in order to fulfill all righteousness (and to please His father), His father commended Him. We need to learn this from our Heavenly Father.

For many of us, it's too late. Our children are grown and gone, however, we can still commend them as adults and our grandchildren when they do well in life. I think the art of commending one another is a must for all of life. It's a "must do" thing.

All of us should want to please our Father. When we're baptized into Christ it pleases our Heavenly Father. When we witness for Christ, invite people to church, demonstrate love to hurting people, etc. we please our

Heavenly Father. And when we give for the cause of Christ or to help some needy person we are also pleasing our Heavenly Father.

My dad was a truck driver. I never wanted to drive a truck. I don't know why, because when I was young I was fascinated with dad's big truck and how well he could drive it and back it into a loading chute. It's just highly possible that one of the finest compliments I could have given him would have been to take more interest in his work and become a truck driver myself.

Probably one of the finest compliments we could give our Heavenly Father would be to take more interest in His work and imitate Him in giving.

V. 19 "And my God will meet all your needs according to his glorious riches in Christ Jesus."

Prov. 3:9-10 "Honor the Lord with your wealth…then your barns will be filled to overflowing…"

Malachi 3:10 "Bring the whole tithe into the storehouse, that there may be food in my house. Test me in this, says the Lord Almighty, and see if I will not throw open the floodgates of heaven and pour out so much blessing that you will not have room enough for it."

II Cor 9:6 "Remember this: whoever sows sparingly will also reap sparingly, and whoever sows generously will also reap generously."

Arnold Schwarzenegger was born on July 30, 1947 as the second child of a police chief in Graz, Austria. He was raised in poverty and was 14 before his family could afford to furnish their home with indoor plumbing, a refrigerator and a telephone.

When Arnold began lifting weights as a teen to train for the local soccer team, he first sensed that he was destined for greatness. At age 15, he set a goal of winning the Mr. Universe weightlifting contest. At age 18, he joined the Austrian army to supplement his weightlifting training diet with fresh meat. One month after enlisting, he went AWOL to compete in the Mr. Junior Europe contest. He went on to win the titles of Junior Mr. Europe, Mr. World, Mr. Universe (five times) and Mr. Olympia (seven times).

Brothers and sisters, Arnold has not always been the Arnold that we know today! He wasn't born with big muscles. It took time and hard work to develop those muscles and that physique.

The point of what I'm saying is this: when you give to the body it gives back to you! I know this is true, because I've proved it to myself. When you give to something, it comes back to you!

This is also very true when it comes to giving away kindness, money, etc.

Prov. 11:24-25 "One man gives freely, yet gains even more; another withholds unduly, but comes to poverty. A generous man will prosper, he who refreshes others will himself be refreshed."

Goodness and kindness will always come back to you! What you sow is what you will reap. God will always take care of those who give to others.

J.L. Kraft, head of the Kraft Cheese Corporation, who had given approximately 25% of his enormous income to Christian causes for many years, said, "The only investment I ever made which has paid consistently increasing dividends is the money I have given to the Lord."

J.D. Rockefeller said, "I never would have been able to tithe the first million dollars I ever made if I had not tithed my first salary, which was $1.50 per week."

I am not suggesting that if we give that God will make us rich people. Not at all, but He has promised that when we give He will provide for us and take care of our needs.

Sermon 9 - Use What God Gives

Did you hear about the city slicker who had always dreamed of owning a cattle ranch? He saved every penny and finally scraped up enough money to buy his dream property. His close friend flew out to visit and asked, "So, what did you use as a name for your ranch?" His buddy told him that he had thought hard to come up with a name that he liked. He and his wife couldn't agree on what to call it so they decided on, "The Double Z Lazy K Triple Horseshoe Bar-9 Lucky Diamond Ranch."

His friend was quite impressed but then asked, "So where are all the cows?" To which the new ranch owner replied, "We had quite a few…but none of them survived the branding!"

I want to suggest to you this morning that like that rancher, it's possible to get so caught up in what we call our spiritual gifts that we might not survive servanthood! The key is not so much to identify what we have but to use what we've been given. 1 Peter 4:10: "Each one should use whatever gift he has received to serve others, faithfully administering God's grace in its various forms."

Let's look at Matthew 25:14-30. Let's set the context. This parable comes in the section of Matthew's gospel where Jesus is giving an answer to the disciples' question about His Second Coming in Matthew 24:3: "...When will this happen, and what will be the sign of your coming and of the end of the age?" Jesus warns them to be on guard so that no one will deceive them and helps them understand that once He leaves, He will come again. He challenges them in Matthew 24:44 to be ready because the Son of Man will come at an hour when He is least expected.

In chapter 25, Jesus compares His coming to the eastern custom of a bridegroom arriving in the middle of the night. He concludes by saying in 25:13: "Therefore, keep watch, because you do not know the day or the hour." Chapter 25 ends with the separation of the sheep and the goats. Sandwiched in-between is the parable of the talents.

Notice verse 14: "Again, it will be like a man going on a journey..." The word "again" indicates that Jesus is using yet one more parable to explain future events. The man going on a "journey" is Jesus.

As we walk through this powerful passage, we'll see Seven Stewardship Lessons.

1What we have is not ours. Verse 14 continues by saying that this man who was getting ready for a journey, "...called his servants and entrusted His property to them." It was common for wealthy men to take long journeys. Before they would leave, they would arrange to have someone pick up their mail and feed their pets. But even more than that, they would often delegate the control and multiplication of their wealth to trustworthy employees. They were expected to bring a return on what had been handed over to them. Given the uncertainties of transportation in those days, the time of return for even a well-planned trip was often open-ended.

There was no doubt in the minds of these servants that the property and money still belonged to the master. They were the possessors, but not the owners. Their job was to manage what they were given. Likewise, we must remember that everything we have has been given to us and is not really ours anyway. Psalm 24:1 says, "The earth is the LORD's, and everything in it, the world, and all who live in it." Haggai 2:8 adds, "The silver is mine and the gold is mine, declares the LORD Almighty." He has the rights, and I have the responsibility. He is the Master and I am the manager. I am the servant; He is the sovereign.

Have you allowed this basic principle to permeate your personhood? You don't really own anything. Everything belongs to the Lord. Until we recognize this truth, we will not be good managers of what has been entrusted to us. Our days are in His hands. Our gifts and abilities are on loan from Him. Our money is an "advance" from the Almighty. Our houses, cars, clothes, and every possession we have doesn't belong to us. We really don't own anything.

2. We're given what we can handle. In verse 15 we see that the master gave some talents to three of his servants: "To one he gave five talents of money, to another two talents, and to another one talent, each according to his ability. Then he went on his journey."

We need to pause here in order to recognize that this word "talent" is different from our present-day understanding. A talent was a measure of weight as used in Revelation 16:21: "From the sky huge hailstones of about a hundred pounds each fell upon men." A talent was also used to indicate a very large sum of money. Its value varied depending on whether it was copper, silver, or gold. While commentators differ on the exact amount, most agree that it would take an ordinary laborer almost twenty years to earn just one talent. To put this into our economy, using a minimal hourly wage, a talent would be the equivalent of about $300,000.

We need to focus on discovering, developing, and deploying of spiritual gifts, this parable has first reference to how we invest our money. It has a secondary application to how we use our God-given talents and supernatural abilities.

That reminds me of two men who crashed their private plane on a South Pacific Island.

One of the men brushed himself off and proceeded to run all over the island to see if they had any chance of survival. When he returned, he rushed up to the other man and screamed, "This Island is uninhabited and there is no food or water. We're going to die!"

The other man leaned back against the fuselage of the wrecked plane, folded his arms and responded, "No we're not. I make over $100,000 a week." The first man grabbed his friend and shook him. "Listen, we're on a deserted island. We're doomed!"

The other man, unruffled, again responded. "It's OK, I make over $100,000 a week." Mystified, the first man, taken aback with such an answer again repeated, "For the last time, I'm telling you that we are lost. It doesn't matter how much money you make because there's no one around to help us." Still unfazed, the first man looked the other guy in the eye and said, "Don't make me say this again. I make over $100,000 per week and I tithe 10%! My pastor will find us!"

Let me put you at ease this morning. I'm not going to preach about tithing except to say that if you make that many shekels a week, I'll track you down somehow!

Let's go back to the story. The Master gave the first servant five talents, which was about $1.5 million. The second guy received two talents, or approximately $600,000. And the third steward got one talent, or $300,000. Even though there's a big difference between five talents and one talent, the guy who received one talent still had a lot of money. That reminds us that God gives out of His abundance to us!

I want you to notice that each servant received talents "according to his ability." Your responsibility is tied to your ability. This is very interesting. God's kingdom purposes do not operate according to what is "fair" but according to what is best. In 1 Corinthians 3:5, after challenging believers to be united by not breaking into subgroups who follow different leaders, Paul writes, "What, after all, is Apollos? And what is Paul? Only servants, through whom you came to believe-as the Lord has assigned to each his task." Did you catch that? Each of us has been assigned a task. It's our job to be faithful to what He has given us to do.

You have what you have because God gave it to you. And He expects you to manage His gifts within the boundaries of ability that He has wired into you. As we learned last week from 1 Corinthians 12, there are different kinds of gifts, service, and workings, and the Holy Spirit distributes these responsibilities "to each one, just as He determines." God entrusts different stuff to different people according to His sovereign purposes. In other words, He knows what we can handle. Our job is to be faithful with whatever amount we have to work with. Do we trust that God knows more about us than we even know about ourselves?

3. We must invest what we've been given. Verse 16 tells us that the man who received five talents went "at once and put his money to work and gained five more." He didn't waste any time but immediately went to work on his investment strategy and doubled his master's portfolio. The guy who got two talents did the same thing; only the text doesn't say he went to work "at once" like the first guy did. We do know that he worked hard however, because he also doubled his master's money, ending up with four talents.

Verse 18 describes the different approach of the third servant: "But the man who had received the one talent went off, dug a hole in the ground and hid his master's money." Even though we don't read about any specific instructions for what to do with the money, the first two guys went to work and multiplied their investment. The one-talent guy was a slacker who went off and buried his blessing. The practice of hiding valuables in the ground was quite common back then. It was one of the safest—and least profitable—ways of protecting possessions.

Because Antonio's voice was high and squeaky, he did not make the tryouts for the Cremona Boy's Choir. When he took violin lessons, the neighbors persuaded his parents to make him stop. Yet Antonio still wanted to make music.

His friends gave him a hard time because his only talent was whittling. When Antonio was older he served as an apprentice to a violinmaker. His knack for whittling grew into a skill of carving and his hobby became his craft. He worked patiently and faithfully. By the time he died, he left over 1,500 violins, each one bearing a label that read, "Antonio Stradivarius." They are the most sought-after violins in the world and sell for more than $100,000 each. Antonio couldn't sing or play or preach or teach but his responsibility was to use his ability, and his violins are still making beautiful music today.

Our potential is God's gift to us. What we do with it is our gift to Him. Zig Ziglar has said, "You are the only person on earth who can use your ability." Are you investing what you've been given, regardless of how much it is? Or, have you buried your blessing and kept it hidden from others?

4. A day of accountability is coming. None of us want to be audited by the IRS, but we'll all be audited by the Almighty. We'll have to give an account for how we've used what we've been given. Look at verse 19: "After a long time the master of those servants returned and

settled accounts with them." Jesus is coming again and there will be a day of reckoning. While most of us believe this in our heads, we don't always live with eternity in our hearts. If we would think more about His return, we'd be more focused on making an eternal return on our investments. Romans 14:12: "So then, each of us will give an account of himself to God." It was the duty of servants to always bear in mind that the master would be returning and would settle his accounts with them.

Friends, Jesus is coming again! Let's be faithful in doing whatever He gives us to do. He's invested something in you, and one day He's coming back to claim it. Your job may be big or small, but whatever it is, do it to the best of your ability and you'll be ready for your audit. Wouldn't it be terrible to be ashamed and unprepared when Jesus comes back? 1 John 2:28: "And now, dear children, continue in Him, so that when He appears we may be confident and unashamed before Him at His coming." Serve in light of a future reckoning.

It would help us to get in the habit of asking the question, "How will my money management, or this decision to serve or not serve look on the day of accountability?"

5. What we do with what we have reveals our view of God. As we come to verses 20-25, we see that the man who had been given five talents brought five more with him. The language is insightful here. He says, "See, I have gained five more." The word "see" means, "Behold" or "Look!" He was eager to invest what he had been given and now he's excited to show the master what He had done. He's bubbling with enthusiasm and thoroughly thrilled. He couldn't wait to present what he had done because he wanted to please the owner.

The man with the two talents approached this time of reckoning with the same anticipation and excitement. The master is thrilled with both of them because they demonstrated responsibility for their ability. He says the exact same thing to both of them: "Well done, good and faithful servants! You have been faithful with a few things; I will put you in charge of many things. Come and share your master's happiness!" The master increased their resources after they had proven themselves faithful. Jesus said a similar thing in Luke 6:38: "Give, and it will be given to you."

These two faithful servants received: Affirmation: "Great job! Well done. I appreciate your good work and your faithfulness."

Promotion: "Since you've done so well with what I've given you, I'm going to give you even more responsibility and opportunity for growth."
Celebration: "You've made me very happy. Let's celebrate together!"
The phrase, "well done" can be translated, "excellent," or "wonderful." They were faithful and were called good because they had a right view of the master. Likewise, when we see God for who He is, we will want to be faithful and we'll focus on doing good things. God is

looking for faithful people, for those who properly manage their resources for kingdom purposes. And, when we're responsible for what we've been given, we'll be given even more responsibilities. I picture a smile on Jesus' face when He says, "Come and share your master's happiness!"

The one-talent guy came a bit more reluctantly to the master and said in verse 24: "…I knew that you were a hard man…" Notice that the first words out of his mouth were about himself: "I knew." We could translate this as, "I always knew." The other two guys kept the focus on the master when he returned: "Master, you entrusted me."

This third guy had a wrong view of the master and had his mind made up even before he received his talent. He looked at him as someone who was hard and harsh, instead of loving and gracious. A.W. Tozer was right when he said that what we think about God is the most important thing about us. If we view God as a tyrant then we'll filter everything through this lens. Some of you may be secretly angry with God because you think He did something, or didn't do something that you think He should have. As a result, your view of Him is skewed. Your preconceived notions prevent you from seeing Him as a God of grace, and as a result you refuse to serve Him with what He's given you. When we blame God we end up burying our blessings.

A faulty view of God can also lead to excuses. In verse 25 this man declares that the reason he didn't do anything with what he had been given was because he was afraid. His fear paralyzed him and so he decided to play it safe. He hid the money to make sure it wouldn't be lost. And he accomplished exactly what he set out to achieve: nothing. Like the saying goes, "If you aim at nothing, you'll hit it every time."

A wrong view of God always leads to fear: "So I was afraid and went out and hid your talent in the ground…" A right view of God always leads to faith. If you're struggling with fear today, the best antidote is to further your understanding of the character of God and ask Him to grow your faith. Courage is not the absence of fear. Courage is moving ahead in spite of your fears. I think the first two guys were probably a little afraid as well, but because they knew the master's character, instead of being frozen by fear, they stepped out in faith.

Let's look at the differences between the two servants who served and the one who took a dive.

The first two were determined to make a profit; the third was determined to not take a loss. The first two were willing to work hard and take risks; the third took no risks.

The first two received the gift; the third refused the gift. The first two wanted to advance the master's domain; the third had no interest in what mattered to the master. The first two viewed the money as an opportunity; the third guy saw it as a problem. The first two allowed the master's gift to change their lives; the third refused to let the gift touch his life. The first two invested; the other one wasted. The first two saw a blessing; the third guy saw a burden.

The first two knew the master; the third guy had no clue.

6. What we have we must use or what we have we will lose. Verse 26 reveals that the master saw right through the flimsy excuses of the servant when he said, "You wicked, lazy servant!" The word "wicked" means "evil, hurtful, and malicious." In other words, the master is saying, "You're lying. In your heart, you are a selfish and lazy bum. If you really wanted to do something, you would have put my money in the bank. I see right through you." These are pretty strong words. God will judge not merely for doing wrong, but for not doing right!

The man was wicked because he deliberately misrepresented both his master and himself. He falsely accused the master of being harsh and he lied when he said in verse 25: "See, here is what belongs to you." He actually owed his employer not only one talent but also whatever it would have earned had he been faithful.

Amazingly, instead of owning his guilt, he behaves as if the master should have given him credit for having been so cautious.

Wickedness and laziness partner together to keep many people from full surrender and service. In the original, this combination of terms is unforgettable because they rhyme. While the other two servants were busy and working hard, this selfish sluggard dug a hole, little realizing that he was digging it for himself! A selfish heart coupled with an unwillingness to do anything about it, will take many people on the path of destruction that can lead to the place of weeping and gnashing of teeth.

We all have an element of laziness in us. And, our culture seems to be set on slothfulness as well. Just this week it was announced that Nintendo is looking to hire 50 people this summer at a wage of $100 a day to play computer games all summer long.

I'm convinced that laziness is extremely dangerous to our spiritual lives. When we think we can put something off until later, we will eventually discover that it will one day be too late.

Proverbs 6:9: "How long will you lie there, you sluggard? When will you get up from your sleep?"

Proverbs 10:5: "He who gathers crops in summer is a wise son, but he who sleeps during harvest is a disgraceful son."

Proverbs 13:4: "The sluggard craves and gets nothing, but the desires of the diligent are fully satisfied."

Hebrews 6:11-12: "We want each of you to show this same diligence to the very end, in order to make your hope sure. We do not want you to become lazy, but to imitate those who through faith and patience inherit what has been promised."

Because this third guy did not use what He had been given, He lost it according to verse 28: "Take the talent from him and give it to the one who has the ten talents." It's the "use it or lose it" principle. Friend, don't hold what you have. Develop it, compound it, and multiply it by using what you've been given.

7. Who you know and what you do will lead to either abundance or agony in the next life. In verse 29, we learn that those who are faithful with the little things will have an abundance, or excess: "For everyone who has will be given more, and he will have an abundance." Those who have given themselves in full surrender and selfless service will be given even more opportunities.

On the other hand, those who bury their blessings will face agony. Jesus concludes this parable by saying that the worthless servant will be thrown "outside, into the darkness, where there will be weeping and gnashing of teeth." This description is used elsewhere to refer to hell. Those who don't know God don't serve Him. A lack of serving may indicate that a person has never been truly converted. That's why Jesus referred to him as "worthless." A believer has worth because of his faith in

Christ. This servant lived in the house of the Master but didn't know and love the owner.

A distinguishing mark of a true Christian is service and giving. A lack of service betrays a heart where Jesus doesn't really live.

A Christian who is not using what God has given is a contradiction in terms. As you survey your servanthood quotient, and you conclude that you've buried your blessings, maybe you haven't yet been saved. Do you want abundance or agony in the next life? Determine to know the Master and serve Him wholeheartedly.

Don't hide the truth. Don't bury it. Allow the greatest treasure of all Jesus Christ Himself to radically reform your life.

Summary:

Stewardship is best defined as the use of God-given resources for the accomplishment of God-given goals. How do you line up with these seven principles?

What we have is not ours. We're given what we can handle.

We must invest what we've been given. A day of accountability is coming. What we do with what we have reveals our view of God.

What we have we must use or what we have we will lose.

Who you know will lead to either abundance or agony in the next life.

Have you ever seen the "Antique Road Show" on TV? I like watching how people bring their stuff to the appraisers to find out how much it's worth. Many times those who have lavish items come on the show thinking that they have a huge treasure. More often than not, they find out their treasure is a forgery or a duplicate and worth very little.

Then there are those who come with a small trinket or a painting that was up in their dusty attic. They're just happy to be on the show. And, many times, these people discover that their item is worth far more than they thought.

The people who are hoping to hit it big with their extravagant item are a bit like we are when we think we can impress God with what we have. On the other hand, some of us think that we don't have much to offer, but what we have is really a treasure from God himself. Our responsibility is to use our ability to invest in God's kingdom purposes.

Jesus has placed His business into our hands and will return someday to judge our faithfulness. Are you partnering with Him or are you making excuses?

Sermon 10 - God's Will for Us

Someone could not be blamed for thinking that God is the promoter of the American dream, especially if you watch many of the TV and radio preachers that are broadcasting today. Indeed, God's plan is sometimes presented as a heavenly casino where instead of spinning a roulette wheel your prayers are like rolling the dice at a craps table. Then if you roll the right number God drops money, cars, houses and spouses upon you and will even cure your aching feet and bad breath to boot!

Promoted ideas include specific formulas, repetitive prayers, anointed prayer cloths or special water that guarantee to bring wealth and blessing upon you direct from God. Some of these things remind me of that old game show, "You Bet Your Life", where if you said the secret word a little bird would drop down and the contestant would win money; only in the case of these "anointed" items or formulas it is God that is magically dispensing the free gifts!

You would think that with all those wonderful things available that the Church today would be loaded with people who are well-heeled and physically healed, yet it appears the contrary is true even in America. You don't have to travel very far to see that most churches are small and the congregations are lower middle class to poor with health issues and that is in America. In many other countries,

It is more like poorer and poorest and the diseases that accompany them are poverty and malnutrition.

So what is the problem? Some would likely explain it away due to a lack of faith of the poor and sick yet James says that it is the prayers of the elders that heals the sick, not the faith or prayer of the afflicted. The man at the Beautiful Gate had no faith. It was Peter's faith in Christ that healed him. The lame man didn't even know what was coming. There are times when healing comes by the faith of the sick as with the crippled man that Paul perceived had faith to be healed but we have the examples of James 5 and Peter's action that show that it is not always the faith of the sick that is needed or fails when healing does not come.

In 3 John, verses 1-2 we read: "The elder unto the well beloved Gaius, whom I love in the truth.

Beloved, I wish above all things that thou mayest prosper and be in health, even as thy soul prospereth.

Some may have said, "See, there you have it! We are to be prosperous and healthy! This is from the disciple Jesus loved so it must be so!" Keeping the passage in context we see that this blessing or well-wishing is directed to an individual, not the Church or an open blessing to all saints. He doesn't even say that it will come to pass. It is John's wish or desire that it happens but it is not a prediction of the future only a hope. We wish people a blessed day or a great day all the time. Does it guarantee that they will have a great day. Sometimes their day will be terrible even though they were "blessed" or wished happiness many times that day.

It is John's heartfelt wish that Gaius prospers, but that doesn't mean immense wealth. If I am a business man and my business sees a 5% profit over last year I have prospered by 2% since the cost of living usually goes up 3% per year. That doesn't mean it is time to retire but I did prosper. To prosper does not mean I will in Highland Park, Beverly Hills or wherever your rich people dwell.

In my doctor's office he has a Power Point presentation that tells about various health issues but also the origin and meanings of various words. Health comes from the Teutonic word for salvation. In an Asian language, crisis comes from the words for danger and opportunity. Enthusiasm comes from the Greek meaning God within. I always find those things interesting. He also has a slide that says health is not being disease free. Indeed, you can be on the borderline between disease and what we call healthy. You can feel great one day and die the next because the line was crossed without any symptoms of sickness. Real health is to be growing and being stronger, not just status quo.

Wouldn't that make a good definition of a healthy spiritual life? That brings us to the caveat or crux of these verses. Note, John's real concern for Gaius was for his soul. He wanted the soul to be prosperous and healthy and tied the blessing to that. As your soul prospers so also may your business and body prosper. It is the inner or spiritual health and prosperity that God really cares about as does John in this passage. As thy soul prospers, Gaius, I wish the other blessings for you as well. Desiring is not giving. He could not give Gaius prosperity of soul then or for the future. He could only desire that his soul continued to prosper and as it did he desired the rest would also be true. Yet, Gaius' soul could not prosper and be in health without the externals keeping up with it.

John could not predict that Gaius would always prosper in his soul. He was doing well right then but do you remember Demas? He was spoken well of in two passages but then something happened and he forsook Paul because this present world became his love object. Why? Was he tired of hanging around Paul in dingy jails and living hand to mouth off the charity of the saints? Paul knew how to abound and to be abased meaning there were some lean times. Did Demas see an opportunity to prosper that he thought would lead to a healthier lifestyle though it would impoverish and sicken his soul? We are not told but perhaps this world had some appeal to him.

Think of all the rich in this world who have the finest physicians and enjoy health and health care in ways we cannot imagine and yet they are unbelievers. There is usually so much in their lives that shows they are critically ill and poverty stricken in their souls. It does not make wealth so appealing. Yet, as you look around the world and maybe even in your own community, you can find people who are fiscally poor and in poor health but who are happy; praising God and talking of being immensely blessed. They are rich with peace, love, joy and the other fruit of the Spirit in their souls and it shows. Whoever took the Teutonic word for salvation and created our word health was completely on target. A saved person dying of any disease is healthier that the most fit lost person.

Wealth does not always bring happiness and certainly cannot guarantee health. I have read of many rich people dying from the same diseases that afflict poor people. I also know of Christians overseas who will never be wealthy and are persecuted by beatings, rapes and murder who are happier than most Christians sitting in their comfortable homes or padded pews. The poorest of our people here are richer than at least 80% of the rest of the world and we are some of the most unhappy and ungrateful people imaginable. Some of our persecuted brethren will risk life and limb to get even a piece of a Bible while we may have a dozen on the shelf unread.

When they are imprisoned they witness to the other prisoners and the guards even if may mean beatings or isolation. Here, we fear to give out a tract or speak to someone about Christ, but have no problems talking about sports teams or some other thing that won't help keep a soul from Hell.

Let us look at the ultimate passage on the subject of wealth and prosperity for the Christian, the Hall of Faith in Hebrews 11.

Hebrews 11:31-40 "By faith the harlot Rahab perished not with them that believed not, when she had received the spies with peace. And what shall I more say? for the time would fail me to tell of Gedeon, and of Barak, and of Samson, and of Jephthae; of David also, and Samuel, and of the prophets: Who through faith subdued kingdoms, wrought righteousness, obtained promises, stopped the mouths of lions, Quenched the violence of fire, escaped the edge of the sword, out of weakness were made strong, waxed valiant in fight, turned to flight the armies of the aliens. Women received their dead raised to life again: and others were tortured, not accepting deliverance; that they might obtain a better resurrection: And others had trial of cruel mockings and scourgings, yea, moreover of bonds and imprisonment: They were stoned, they were sawn asunder, were tempted, were slain with the sword: they wandered about in sheepskins and goatskins; being destitute, afflicted, tormented; (Of whom the world was not worthy:) they wandered in deserts, and in mountains, and in dens and caves of the earth. And these all, having obtained a good report through faith, received not the promise: God having provided some better thing for us, that they without us should not be made perfect.

When you read verses 31 up to 35, you could jump up and down and shout, "See! It's victory and glory for us! David was a king and rich. Some of those dudes lived very well." Yes, but as Paul Harvey was known to say, let's look at "the rest of the story." After that verse, life gets a tad bit different for those listed in God's Hall of Fame for the

Faithful. We all like to claim the Word and identify with a biblical character when the words are victory and blessings. Is anyone going to start asking God to make them like the folks from mid verse 35 to verse 38? I doubt it.

Did these folks have faith? You bet or they would not be in this passage. But where is the power, riches, blessings, etc? Yes, how about that? I guess it isn't a universal rule that all God's children are going to have so much stuff they have to buy sheds or rent storage space. They don't all have so many clothes they cannot decide what to wear or get bored with after a few months. Nope, sometimes God's children don't get their reward until they get home to Heaven.

I know there is a scribe or lawyer somewhere that will point out that these people are all Old Testament saints. Well, OK. John the Baptist lost his head, but then he would be classified as the last Old Testament prophet. Hmm, Stephen was stoned for his witness. James was killed by a government sword and it was a Roman ax that made Paul lose his head. Tradition says that all the rest of the Apostles also met an untimely end save John who was exiled to Patmos after boiling him in oil failed to kill him.

It is amazing that none of the Apostles grasped the wealth and health doctrines since apparently they taught it as the modern day lads are using their epistles to espouse those doctrines. Yet, the Apostle Paul Ministries (APM) were not headquartered in Ephesus where Paul left his five million denarius house to travel to the Christian Cathedral of Prosperity in his twenty-horse gilded chariot to preach to thousands on how Christ came that they also may have marble toilets in their offices. What were the Apostles thinking or where was their faith since they did not latch on to their birthright?

What shall we say about all the martyrs since the 1st Century? Were they all faithless twits that did not know it was their destiny to be rich and healthy instead of martyrs? We need to make sure we get the word to our brethren in other lands to stop denying their birthright and allowing people to torture and kill them for their faith. They need to name and claim their wealth and health and expect a miracle other than escaping captivity or surviving in horrible prison conditions. Send them crates of prayer cloths, anointed amulets and special water! Oh, yes, I suppose we should send them bibles but more than that all the books by the great messengers of the new apostolic reformation.

Balderdash to all that! It is better to be bankrupt in this world and rich in the next than the other way around. Seek true riches that will last for eternity. No matter what you amass here you will either leave it to people who will most likely waste it or it will be burned up to make way for the new heaven and new earth. If we want true wealth and riches then we need to heed the injunctions of 1 Timothy 6 and other passages speaking to the errors of loving money and desiring unrighteous mammon. These are in direct conflict with the heresies being taught by the most popular speakers. Paul commands us to stay away from them for their teachings are...1 Tim 6:5-9

5 Perverse disputings of men of corrupt minds, and destitute of the truth, supposing that gain is godliness: from such withdraw thyself.

6 But godliness with contentment is great gain.

7 For we brought nothing into this world, and it is certain we can carry nothing out.

8 And having food and raiment let us be therewith content.

9 But they that will be rich fall into temptation and a snare, and into many foolish and hurtful lusts, which drown men in destruction and perdition.

If you are unsaved today all the wealth in the world will not help you even if you die in your sleep of old age. You will lose your soul in Hell for eternity just like the rich man in Luke. If you are broke but saved then you have more wealth than you can imagine and even if you are physically ill here one day you will be in perfect condition living with your Savior forever.

Maybe you are sick because you have fallen into the trap of coveting wealth and this economy is not helping you achieve your goals and even setting you so far back you will never reach them. Work on prospering your soul and seeking the health that will bring about as you turn over your goals to Christ and being happy that you have food, clothes and even shelter which Paul does not mention. Don't worry and covet stuff that will burn up but seek the gold, silver and precious stones that will survive the fire at the Bema seat because they were created from a life lived in holiness and in fellowship with Christ. Behold He cometh quickly! Glory to God!

Sermon 11 - Prosperity from God

No matter what situation you may be in right now, you know for a fact that God is great, and He is able and willing to meet all our needs. Now if you're like me, you may notice sometimes that it seems like God has a strange way of dealing with us.

From 1 Kings 17 you can read about a person who was extremely destitute, without anything and even without the hope of anything; it was the poor widow, who ended up having an amazing encounter with God. She might have been destitute, but in her lack, God sent the prophet Elijah, to demonstrate God's intervention through His provision. God's ways oftentimes seem to "surprise" us. We do not always understand what He is up to, nor do we understand how He does things in a way that would benefit us in the end.

In the Gospel, you will see Jesus talking to a tree, or commanding Peter to get their tax payment from the mouth of the fish, or putting saliva on the soil that produced the mud that healed the blind man's eyes. He walked on water and turned water into wine! In 1 Kings 17, we can see how God can meet our needs, not by ways known to man, but by "His" ways.

God used the raven. How about a raven to supply your food today?

Matthew Henry's commentary said and I quote:

"God could have sent angels to minister to him; but he chose to show that he can serve his own purposes by the meanest creatures, as effectually as by the mightiest".

From a human's point of view, a raven is certainly not the most likely or qualified creature to bring one's daily of supply of food. On the contrary, ravens are scavengers. I believe God purposely chose this ugly bird to be the instrument of His provision to prevent Elijah from idolizing it as the source of His provision.

Sometimes, we Christians easily put our trust on the "messenger" rather than the "Giver." Unwittingly, we sometimes slowly put our faith on the instrument of provisions rather than on the Provider Himself. We trust in the job, the pension instead of the true source, God Himself.

God uses the widow, Verse 17 reads: "Go at once to Zarephath of Sidon and stay there. I have commanded a widow in that place to supply you with food."God's commands do not always appeal to our intellect, while in fact, they are the most logical things to do! God uses the humble individual more often than He uses the mighty to support His work.

One of the most destitute person who lived on earth is the widow - she had nothing ; no property of her own. Every time the bible speaks of a widow – it is always a picture of a poor individual.

In 1Corinthians 1:27b, God chose the weak things of the world to shame the strong.

In Matthew Henry's commentary, he said and I quote: The widow appointed to entertain Elijah is not one of the rich or great men of Sidon; but a poor widow, in want, and desolate, is made both able and willing to sustain him. It is God's way, and it is his glory, to make use of, and put honor upon the weak and foolish things of the world.

I believe God did this on purpose to teach Elijah total dependence on God alone, whenever he is in need.

God can sometimes challenge us with seemingly "difficult" things. He sometimes will tell us to give more out of the little that we have.

Most of my testing in giving happened when I had meager resources.

(Verses 10,11) – So he went to Zarephath. When he came to the town gate, a widow was there gathering sticks. He called to her and asked, "Would you bring me a little water in a jar so I may have a drink?" As she was going to get it, he called, "And bring me, please, a piece of bread."

(Verse 12) "As surely as the LORD your God lives," she replied, "I don't have any bread—only a handful of flour in a jar and a little oil in a jug. I am gathering a few sticks to take home and make a meal for myself and my son, that we may eat it—and die."

As a pastor, receiving a gift from someone who I feel is in greater need than I am, tears my heart apart. It is out of their genuine selflessness and love for God's work that they are able to do this.

One time, after receiving a love gift from a needy person, my immediate and natural reflex was to "return to sender!" I thought I was doing a rightfully noble thing, until it came to the knowledge of my wife. And this statement which my wife told me, changed my attitude towards receiving gifts. She said that by returning their love gift, I have just "robbed" this person the opportunity to be blessed!

(Verse 15) She went away and did as Elijah had told her...

Pure lack is not an excuse not to give.

(2Corinthians 8: 2-3) Out of the most severe trial, their overflowing joy and their extreme poverty welled up in rich generosity. For I testify that they gave as much as they were able, and even beyond their ability entirely on their own...

Some Christians remain in the state of lack because of their unwillingness to trust God in the area of giving. If that is your attitude today, then be prepared to get stuck in that situation until you can change.

(Verse 16) For the jar of flour was not used up and the jug of oil did not run dry, in keeping with the word of the LORD spoken by Elijah.

As the lyrics of the song goes: "Little becomes much, when you place it in the master's hand".

God sometimes challenges our faith in order for us to experience the supernatural. If we always move in the confines of what is natural and reasonable, then we will never see God's miraculous work in the thick of our circumstances. If the widow ate everything she had, she and her son would have died of starvation.

Many blessings come through trials. Many may have missed their rewards out of sheer lack of trust – giving up long before they have even accepted the challenge placed before them. Giving up long before their "time" has been declared "over!"

In closing, it should be very evident from the story of the widow how God , can at any moment change our situations from an almost "empty" state to an endless overflow of His blessings. Even when we think that He does not understand our situation, He is always there and is able and willing to rescue us from destitution. God is the God of increase! And when He blesses us, He adds no sorry to it! Amen.

Sermon 12 - Prosperity Perspective

The Place of Prosperity in a life of Faith. 1 Timothy 6:3-21

Today I would like us to examine 1 Timothy Chapter 6 and verses 3 to 21. In this portion of scripture the Apostle Paul deals with the topic of the Church's attitude towards Possessions.

The Bible abounds with warnings and exhortations about the dangers of confusing material prosperity with the blessings of God.

Paul wrote in Philippians 4:11-13 "Not that I speak in regard to need, for I have learned in whatever state I am, to be content:(12) I know how to be abased, and I know how to abound. Everywhere and in all things I have learned both to be full and to be hungry, both to abound and to suffer need. (13) I can do all things through Christ who strengthens me."

Solomon who is considered to be the wisest man who ever lived wrote of the danger of greed in Ecclesiastes 5:10, "He who loves silver will not be satisfied with silver; Nor he who loves abundance, with increase."

Yet in spite of the biblical warning the church has been discredited down through the years many times because of greed. In the Middle Ages it was the disgraceful sale of indulgences; a few years ago is was exposure of television evangelists extravagant lifestyles; today it can be cults who charge exorbitant rates for tuition to attain a higher level of spirituality or prosperity preachers who promise personal prosperity to those who will send in "seed money."

You can hear the danger of perverting the truth about prosperity. (A Warning to the False Teachers) In the following passage:

"If anyone teaches otherwise and does not consent to wholesome words, even the words of our Lord Jesus Christ, and to the doctrine which accords with godliness, he is proud, knowing nothing, but is obsessed with disputes and arguments over words, from which come envy, strife, reviling, evil suspicions, useless wranglings of men of corrupt minds and destitute of the truth, who suppose that godliness is a means of gain. From such withdraw yourself.

The first mark of a false teacher is that they deviate from the truth. (v. 3) "If anyone teaches otherwise and does not consent to wholesome words, even the words of our Lord Jesus Christ, and to the doctrine which accords with godliness." There will be those who come advocating a different doctrine (heteros – different, disaskaleo – teaching). In order to be able to identify error we don't need to study the teaching of every cult we need to be well grounded in the truth. Just as in the detection of counterfeit money, the best method to identify the counterfeit teaching, is to become familiar with the real deal. Two essential marks of sound teaching are that they come from Christ and they promote godliness! The second mark of a false teacher is that they divide the church (vv. 4-5a).

"He is proud, knowing nothing, but is obsessed with disputes and arguments over words, from which come envy, strife, reviling, evil suspicions, useless wranglings of men of corrupt minds and destitute of the truth…" The false teacher is characterized as "proud and knowing nothing" or as the New English Bible puts it he is a "pompous ignoramus." The false teacher has is obsessed (literally has a sick interest) in controversies and quarrels about words.

The third mark of a false teacher is that in the final analysis they love money. "… who suppose that godliness is a means of gain."

There is also a danger of worshipping prosperity.

"Now godliness with contentment is great gain. For we brought nothing into this world, and it is certain we can carry nothing out. And having food and clothing, with these we shall be content. But those who desire to be rich fall into temptation and a snare, and into many foolish and harmful lusts which drown men in destruction and perdition. For the love of money is a root of all kinds of evil, for which some have strayed from the faith in their greediness, and pierced themselves through with many sorrows."

What these verses teach us is that greed is a trap, for the rich and for the poor and for everyone in between.

"A survey of 2,000 people in the U.S. labor force was conducted to determine how their faith influences their spending. It found, faith makes little difference to the ways in which people actually conduct their financial affairs."

We buy more than we can afford because we want more than we need. Some-one has said that credit cards let you start at the bottom and dig yourself a hole. "How many of you received at least one credit card offer this past week?" The average American receives 32 credit card offers per year, regardless of their credit history.

Nationally, the average American has four major credit cards with an average credit card debt of $9000.00. When you realize that a number of these individuals have been convinced to pay a minimum payment plan, you have a recipe for disaster. A credit card with a balance of $3900.00 making a 3% payment would require nearly 42 years to pay off the debt and the total of those monthly payments would total $14,530.00.

Paul says godliness is 'gain' even 'great gain' providing you mean spiritual gain and not financial.

The love of money is identified as "a root of all kinds of evil," not the root of all evil. What are the danger signs of loving money? John MacArthur in his commentary identifies five danger signs of loving money.

(1) Those who love money are more concerned with making it than being honest. (2) Those who love

money never have enough of it. (3) Those who love money tend to flaunt it. (4) Those who love money resent giving any away. (5) Those who love money often sin to get it.

Paul reminds Timothy that some people who have become so caught up in their desire for wealth that they have "strayed from the faith," with painful results. The phrase "pierced themselves" literally means to be skewered from every direction and roasted like a piece of meat.

There is also a danger of identifying with prosperity. (A Warning to the Man of God) (vv. 11-16)

"But you, O man of God, flee these things and pursue righteousness, godliness, faith, love, patience, gentleness. Fight the good fight of faith, lay hold on eternal life, to which you were also called and have confessed the good confession in the presence of many witnesses."

In (vv. 11-12) we find four successive commands directed to the child of God; Flee, Follow, Fight and Fasten onto.

"Flee" -"But you, O man of God, flee these things …" What are 'these things" that he is told to flee? He is to flee from the things that characterize the lives of the false teachers. He is to flee any teaching that robs Christ of his glory (v.3). He is to flee from those who are obsessed with fruitless argumentation. He is to flee those who imagine that "godliness is a means to financial gain" (v. 5).

"Follow" – "… and pursue righteousness, godliness, faith, love, patience, gentleness. (v. 11) The Christian life is not just one of flight it is also one pursuit of spiritual virtues. There are here three pairs given here; righteousness-godliness, faith–love, patience–gentleness.

"Fight" – "Fight the good fight of faith, (v. 12a). Earlier in 1:18 Paul had said "wage a good warfare or fight the good fight" where the image was of a soldier but here when he uses (agonizomai) it is suggestive of an athletic contest.

"Fasten onto" – "... lay hold on eternal life, to which you were also called and have confessed the good confession in the presence of many witnesses. (v. 12b) As a believer Timothy already has eternal life, what he is instructed to do is, to grab it for all it worth, to live it to its fullest.

Paul strengthens his appeal to Timothy, with strong arguments of the presence of God and the Second Coming of Christ. In verse thirteen he writes, "I urge you in the sight of God who gives life to all things, and before Christ Jesus who witnessed the good confession before Pontius Pilate, that you keep this commandment without spot, blameless until our Lord Jesus Christ's appearing, which He will manifest in His own time, He who is the blessed and only Potentate, the King of kings and Lord of lords, who alone has immortality, dwelling in unapproachable light, whom no man has seen or can see, to whom be honor and everlasting power. Amen."

Paul's call upon the Father and the Son as witnesses is not meant to intimidate Timothy but rather to encourage him. For in these verses we are given four truths about God's nature and power.

First, God is Invincible. "... He who is the blessed and only Potentate, the King of kings and Lord of lords." (v. 15b). Beyond all earthly power is Jesus who alone has the right to the title – "King of kings and Lord of lords."

Second, God is Immortal. "who alone has immortality..." (v. 16a) which is to say who alone is immoral by nature. It is true that as human being we are immortal in the sense that we survive death, but God alone has life within himself.

Third, God is Inaccessible. "... dwelling in unapproachable light." (v16b)

Fourth, God is Invisible. "... whom no man has seen or can see..." (v. 16c) Being by nature invisible, man can only come to know him so far as it pleases him to make himself known. No one has ever really seen Him, they have only been allowed to see his "glory." (Exodus 24:9, Isaiah 6:1, Ezekiel 1:28).

There is a danger of trusting prosperity. (A Warning to the Rich) (vv. 17-19)

"Command those who are rich in this present age not to be haughty, nor to trust in uncertain riches but in the living God, who gives us richly all things to enjoy. Let them do good, that they be rich in good works, ready to give, willing to share, storing up for themselves a good foundation for the time to come, that they may lay hold on eternal life."

Paul identifies two very real dangers to which the wealthy are exposed. First there is the danger of pride (v. 17a) "Command those who are rich in this present age not to be haughty." Riches have the propensity to make the possessor look down on those less fortunate than themselves.

The second danger is false security

(v. 17) "Command those who are rich in this present age not to …. trust in uncertain riches but in the living God, who gives us richly all things to enjoy."

Final Words to Timothy (vv. 20-21)

"O Timothy! Guard what was committed to your trust, avoiding the profane and idle babblings and contradictions of what is falsely called knowledge—by professing it some have strayed concerning the faith."

You can easily see that by taking in the full counsel of scripture, the believer will receive a balanced perspective on prosperity; to the glory of God. Amen.

Afterword

Thank you for downloading these sermons and sermon notes. You may freely use these and modify them for your own purpose as needed. Please consider to add the following to your library or send a gift copy to a friend or loved one.

To send a gift copy you only need the recipients email address and the gift you give could have a lasting positive impact on their life!

The Complete Words of Jesus

http://www.amazon.com/Complete-Words-Jesus-Only-ebook/dp/B008ADFN10

Is Heaven for Real? Personal Stories of Visiting Heaven

http://www.amazon.com/dp/B00BXKG41U

~ Blessings to you,

Patrick Doucette